T0320442

Team Intelligence

If you have wondered about mesmerizing patterns of flying birds and fish, and asked how they do it, then you have observed what biologists refer to as an intelligent swarm. It is as if the members of the swarm are receiving commands on what to do. It is magic! In reality, it is an intriguing set of behaviors that many species, including birds, fish, bats, wolves, honeybees, termites, and many others, have learned during their millions of years of evolution, which has enabled them to succeed better and sustain their lives.

We have learned and applied our learning from nature and have been inspired to invent many things we use from this fabulous source: Mother Nature! The question that led to extensive research and ultimately to this book may seem strange and unique: Can we use nature for managing people and teams in companies? After all, social beings in nature seem to function very well, and recent research has revealed great approaches they take to make decisions and work together.

This book opens that exact interdisciplinary field, a bridge between managing teams and people in companies, with how similar problems are solved in intelligent swarms. The research supporting this idea has led to a set of principles that will transform traditional teams into Intelligent Teams. These teams are capable of bringing the performance, learning, and happiness of the team members to a new high level.

Security, Audit and Leadership Series

Series Editor: Dan Swanson

Dan Swanson and Associates, Ltd., Winnipeg, Manitoba, Canada.

The *Security, Audit and Leadership Series* publishes leading-edge books on critical subjects facing security and audit executives as well as business leaders. Key topics addressed include Leadership, Cybersecurity, Security Leadership, Privacy, Strategic Risk Management, Auditing IT, Audit Management and Leadership

The CISO Playbook
Andres Andreu

Leveraging Blockchain Technology
Governance, Risk, Compliance, Security, and Benevolent Use Cases
Shaun Aghili

The Closing of the Auditor's Mind?
How to Reverse the Erosion of Trust, Virtue, and Wisdom in Internal Auditing
David J. O'Regan

Radical Reporting
Writing Better Audit, Risk, Compliance, and Information Security Reports (Second Edition)
Sara I. James

Team Intelligence
A New Method Using Swarm Intelligence for Building Successful Teams
Mohammad Nozari

For more information about this series, please visit: https://www.routledge.com/Internal-Audit-and-IT-Audit/book-series/CRCINTAUDITA

Team Intelligence

A New Method Using Swarm Intelligence for Building Successful Teams

Dr. Mohammad Nozari, Ph.D.

CRC Press
Taylor & Francis Group
Boca Raton London New York

CRC Press is an imprint of the
Taylor & Francis Group, an **informa** business

Cover image credit: Mohammad Nozari

First edition published 2025
by CRC Press
2385 NW Executive Center Drive, Suite 320, Boca Raton FL 33431

and by CRC Press
4 Park Square, Milton Park, Abingdon, Oxon, OX14 4RN

CRC Press is an imprint of Taylor & Francis Group, LLC

© 2025 Taylor & Francis Group, LLC

ISBN: 978-1-032-84236-3 (hbk)
ISBN: 978-1-032-86362-7 (pbk)
ISBN: 978-1-003-52720-6 (ebk)

DOI: 10.1201/9781003527206

Typeset in Sabon
by Apex CoVantage, LLC

To Nastaran, for her constant love and support;

And to my future scientists: Yasaman, Rose, and James

Contents

PART 4
Intelligent Team Toolkit   103

Preface

Based on my research, teams can achieve the highest performance possible when they follow certain rules and behaviors that can be learned from social beings in nature. These social beings have been perfecting their methods through millions of years of evolution. Humans haven't had that much time to work together, so we must learn from Mother Nature. Biomimicking, the process of learning from nature, has been used by many inventors, engineers, and scholars; however, for the first time, I invite you to consider what we can learn from nature in better collaboration in teamwork in our companies. The patterns and behaviors I observed by studying the social beings can be transformed into a short list of rules of conduct, team best practices, and organizational setups that can result in high-performing teams. This book is an introduction to many future possibilities that bring the power of nature into the ways of working in today's complex business world.

I call the team that works based on the principles of intelligent swarms an Intelligent Team. Such a team can often follow simple yet effective approaches and techniques used by social beings in nature to achieve similar success.

The book has been divided into four parts. In Part 1, I introduce the concepts and provide the background of my work. I explore the potential high performance of Intelligent Teams that can only materialize when they are properly and differently set up from traditional manager-led teams. I use biomimicking as a unique and untapped resource to achieve that potential to understand how we can draw parallels between our formal existing approaches to teamwork and how it's done in nature.

In Part 2, I introduce the concepts of self-management and intelligent swarms. I provide many examples of how social beings like bees, fish, and birds work together to achieve seemingly impossible results, implying a higher intelligence (hence the term *swarm intelligence*). Then, I use these findings to show how similar self-management teams can be with collaborations in natural swarms, and from there, I start to establish behaviors that can be applied to this new concept, an Intelligent Team that fully applies those principles.

Part 3 contains details of the research I did to show that teams that actually follow more of the Intelligent Team principles are more successful. The research helped to solidify the principles of intelligent swarms and Intelligent Teams into a set of simple rules that can help the team and, as a result, the company to function better. The final part, Part 4, presents a toolkit for leaders to set up intelligent teams and sections on overcoming potential challenges, as well as recommended basic training to prepare team members to work in such settings.

About the Author

Mohammad Nozari is a passionate, energetic, and seasoned scholar-practitioner, researcher, author, and professor. He is also a result-oriented expert who has led and managed strategy development, organizational transformations, implementation, delivery, and maintenance of technology solution with more than 25 years of proven record of service excellence.

A software engineer and computer scientist by education, Mohammad holds an MBA degree in leadership with honors and distinction from the University of Liverpool. His academic education culminated in a PhD in Management, Information Systems from Walden University, where he pioneered a new interdisciplinary field using biomimicking of intelligent swarms and management of teams. As an effective collaborator and network builder, Mohammad is resilient, persuasive, and sensitive to situations and individuals. He knows how to work within the internal and external organization structure in global settings while achieving high degrees of cultural intelligence.

Mohammad is an expert in developing and implementing strategies for reducing operating expenses through demonstrated capabilities in budget and capital planning. He has led a wide range of evaluation and selection of alternative solutions and partners to build efficiency and balance in costs and acceptable risks.

With solid experience in multiple industries, including fintech, health, back-office, automation, control, and telecommunications, Mohammad has a strong passion for education as the essential tool for making positive social change in society. He brings all his experience in teaching courses combining academics and practice. Mohammad has taught at various universities and colleges (including York University in Toronto) in the areas of technology, project management, leadership, and communications. The diversity of his experience allows Mohammad to use a wide range of examples about running businesses, managing situations, and leading initiatives.

He is a proponent of mentoring students in colleges and universities, as well as supporting co-op programs.

Mohammad has written and published papers and books in technology and management, including books on software development, networks, and leadership. He continues his management, leadership, and technology research, combining them with biology, history, and industrial design.

Mohammad's hobbies include reading books, 3D design and printing, and robotics.

EXPERIENCE

Mohammad has held various leadership positions in organizations such as BlackBerry, RBC, CIBC, and BMO, as well as start-up companies in technology. He has a passion for improving the efficiency of technological advancements without losing focus on technologists and the human side of work. Mohammad has managed global and virtual teams in Canada, Ireland, the United States, and India. He has been instrumental in developing processes and organizational units such as Project Management Offices (PMOs) and implementing corporate strategies.

Mohammad has taught at universities and colleges in Iran and Canada. In recent years, he has taught different courses at Seneca College and York University, focusing on project management programs, and delivered a diverse range of courses, including communications, leadership, scheduling, budget management, Agile, and delivery.

With deep knowledge of management science, strategy execution, and information systems, Mohammad has multiple publications in computer software and project management. His recent book titled *Art of Leadership Through Battles* combines his passion for history with leadership and strategy execution.

Part 1

Teamwork

Chapter 1

Introduction

This book establishes a new interdisciplinary field between management/leadership and biomimicking. It is based on my research back in 2018–2020 as a part of my PhD dissertation. As a result of that research, I showed that we can use what we learn from social beings and their behavior and apply them in the management and leadership of companies.

The notion of mimicking other life-forms is not new. *Homo sapiens* have been observing and learning from animals for thousands of years. In Greek mythology, Icarus and his father, Daedalus, were imprisoned by King Minos. Daedalus was a master craftsman. Using feathers and wax, he made two sets of wings. They fly away, but Icarus becomes complacent and flies too close to the sun despite his father's warnings. The wax melts and brings him to his demise (Figure 1.1).

We do not need to go back to Greek mythology to see how much we mimic nature. Examples include Leonardo Da Vinci's flying machine design based on bat wings (Figure 1.2), replicating dragonflies' body form to stabilize helicopter flying, and building modern locomotives inspired by the Kingfisher bird's beak, and so on.

Beyond inspirations to model new inventions and push the boundaries of performance and optimization, we have been watching how animals behave, explicitly to be able to understand and explain why they do what they do and implicitly to apply their behavior wherever possible. There have been many studies and books over the last centuries, even before Darwin's trips and observations, that led to his evolution theory. As Darwin stated, "Everything in nature is a result of fixed laws." The question then becomes, what are these fixed laws? Animals behave instinctively, which means the behaviors have been engraved in their DNA. We do have similar engravings, such as fear of nights, as it brought night dwellers and hunters when we were not able to see them, or jumping at a loud sound, as it is usually followed by a stronger predator chasing us.

It seems though that many of the species can work together and demonstrate high levels of coordination doing so. When we look at the sky and see flocks of birds forming fascinating swarms that, from our standpoint, seem as if something is leading them all, as if there is another entity guiding them

Figure 1.1 Jacob Peter Gowy's *The Flight of Icarus* (1635–1637)

in their flight – same as schools of fish swimming together for protection or prey. How do they do that? When a swarm demonstrates attributes of a higher entity that seems to lead all the members, we call that an intelligent swarm. That intelligence provides protection and sustenance and is a result of millions of years of evolution.

The next question is the nature of swarm intelligence. How do members of an intelligent swarm communicate with each other? How does the swarm work? Research shows, and as Darwin had indicated, there are fixed and simple rules. Each member follows a set of simple rules, and the result is what we see as a higher level of intelligence that goes beyond individuals or groups and encapsulates the whole flock. We will look at some of these simple rules throughout the book and see how we can extract rules of conduct for ourselves to be able to work together better, which is the ultimate goal of this book.

Why now? Many things we know today are quite recent and have been made possible by new digital technologies and Artificial Intelligence (AI). Video technologies have enabled scientists to trace the movements of each

Figure 1.2 Da Vinci's flying machine design

member of the swarm and interpret them. Recent advancements in AI sound technologies have led to the learning new aspects about many species, like bats and elephants. Bats have an extremely complicated and advanced set of sounds that they use to recognize their family, ask for food, and warn of danger. Elephants have words for many things, including "gentle human," "aggressive human," honeybee, and so on. In fact, a dictionary of elephant words is under development, and in the near future, a conversation may be possible!

Finally, you may ask, are you really going to compare complex humans with mere animals? For most of the book, I stick to extremely simple behaviors, so complexity is not an issue. However, recently, we have learned that animals exhibit many behaviors previously deemed unique to humans, including frustration, jealousy, and holding grudges (the latter one, as recent as a study in 2022, observed in bats).

Chapter 2

Self-Organization/ Self-Management

In order to examine what we can learn from intelligent swarms, I will establish the initial parameters that are supported by biologist field researchers and my own research, which proved that teamwork based on biomimicking principles and patterns generates better results. In other words, a team that follows behavioral patterns in social animals can, in fact, get their work done better, stay happier, and enjoy the growth rewards both professionally and financially.

To keep this as close as possible to proven research in the field and to start from a common point of view on the behavior of social beings, whether in the animal kingdom or among smart human beings in a company together, I will have to introduce another concept here, which I alluded to in the first chapter: self-organization or its simpler counterpart, self-management.

When you look at a school of fish swimming together so elegantly or a flock of birds flying so mysteriously in the sky, you are observing a self-organized phenomenon. Through millions of years of evolution, the fish or the birds have learned that when they do this, they benefit in different ways, including safety and easier access to food, but the point is that they do not have a leader. No single bird orchestrates those flight patterns.

Even the famous colony insects don't have a leader when reacting to an attack or damaged nests. Each termite, ant, and honeybee knows what to do. The queens in these colonies have the key role of egg-laying, but they don't command the attack on intruders or have a say in choosing a new location for the nest. As we will see later in this book, they somehow know what to do and, in doing so, demonstrate a fascinating orchestrated effort.

In companies, people come together and work to achieve goals that would be impossible otherwise. Traditionally, there are hierarchies in companies: workers report to managers, and those managers to higher authorities, all the way up to the owner or chief executive officer. In recent years, however, company leaders have concluded that if they give authority to teams, they'll get better results. Many companies have established various types of self-managed teams. They may be called by that name or other terms like "tiger teams," "special-project teams," and so on. Whatever the name, these teams are given the authority to manage themselves, with minimal to no external

    DOI: 10.1201/9781003527206-3

supervision, just a set of goals to achieve. There is no hierarchy; everyone is a team member, regardless of their official titles. In Information Technology (IT), these teams are called Agile teams, which, of course, depending on the organization's understanding of Agile methodology, have variations in the implementation of processes. More and more companies are moving toward implementing self-managed teams, and many have applied the same principles to whole business units or even entire organizations, thus establishing self-managed organizations.

A self-managed team is one with members who receive minimum guidance and influence from higher levels of management in activities such as planning, organizing, and controlling. Corporate leaders want to benefit from the potential advantages of self-managed teams. Many leaders establish self-managed teams to improve innovation, speed, and employee satisfaction. Leaders who lack proper strategies for setting up self-managed teams can create unresolved workplace issues and conflicts and cause a reduction in performance.

The base of this book is research I did as an interdisciplinary view of self-management through the lens of biomimicking (applying the behavior of social beings in nature). This approach can provide a framework that employers use to address the gap in the overall method of implementing self-managed teams with the use of swarm intelligence: suitable decision-making approaches and behaviors learned from other social beings.

Results from this qualitative descriptive multiple case study provide recommendations for employers to consider in solving the decision-making challenges they encounter when implementing self-managed teams. Employers can also discover optimized approaches in other areas of management. Solving self-managed team challenges will lead more employers to adopt these teams, improve employee satisfaction and work-life balance, and may lead to positive social changes in companies with self-managed teams.

BACKGROUND

Leaders of organizations divide their resources into smaller business units or teams to better analyze the organization's mission, formulate actions, plan activities, and monitor progress toward organizational goals. Team size depends on many factors, including organizational size and functions within the organization, but on average, teams can have as few as two members and up to hundreds. Most of the teams observed in the research had 3 to 10 members. In any team design, there are various aspects such as tasks, team dynamics, hierarchy, leadership, accountability, and authority. In a traditional team, a single leader or manager makes the decisions, assigns tasks, and performs planning activities. Self-managed team members have full authority over team activities, including planning, organizing, and decision-making.

Leaders of many organizations create self-managed teams to gain the expected benefits such as higher team performance and employee engagement; however, not all of them have successfully implemented self-managed teams. Since the earliest references to self-organization in the 1960s, corporate leaders have implemented different forms of self-managed teams with mostly positive but inconsistent results. Organizations with effective self-managed teams have higher performance levels, cost savings, innovation, customer satisfaction, commitment, and motivation. However, members of self-managed teams encounter different or similar but augmented challenges than members of traditional teams such as dealing with authority, hierarchy, decision-making, and groupthink. Leaders who understand the drawbacks of self-managed teams allow for the recognition of potential challenges and set the right expectations for self-managed team members. These leaders provide team members with opportunities and tailored solutions rather than traditional approaches. In other words, leaders should recognize that setting up successful self-managed teams requires special setups, in preparing both the team members and organizational elements.

How leaders organize and implement self-managed teams impacts the success or failure of team members. Leaders must organize and set up team design, employee interactions, conflict management, and communications differently for self-managed teams than for traditional teams. However, due to a gap in the literature, a lack of standards in the industry, and improper planning/implementation on how to resolve these differences with an implementation approach, many organizational leaders achieve inconsistent or nonexistent results with self-managed teams.

There have been many researchers to contribute to self-management success. One showed that leaders must establish different teamwork rules to successfully implement self-managed teams. Other researchers have focused on moving to a flatter hierarchy to have better organizational support for self-managed teams. Another research found that managers need new leadership elements to support self-managed teams and examined the level of trust leaders need to allow successful implementation of self-managed teams. Although these studies presented how leaders can successfully implement self-managed teams, there is a shortage of research on the core decision-making differences between self-managed teams and traditional teams.

Members in self-managed teams must engage in decision-making processes as the traditional role of the manager to make the decisions does not apply. Team members who are closer to the underlying elements of a situation make the decisions in self-managed teams. However, members of self-managed teams may struggle to make high-quality decisions due to issues such as groupthink and concerted control. In groupthink, a few vocal participants dominate the discussion and guide team members accordingly, diminishing the input from others and potentially causing missed opportunities (Janis, 1971). Members of self-managed teams may have increased problems with groupthink due to a lack of enforcement from external leaders. Organizational leaders could streamline the implementation of self-managed teams if they provided self-managed team members with tailored decision-making approaches.

So far, I've established that (a) self-managed teams can produce better results, (b) to do this, leaders have to set up self-managed teams, and (c) it's not that easy to establish self-managed teams due to the conflict between the concept of self-management and the existing traditional hierarchical mindset. Now, let's see how Mother Nature can help.

Humans learn from nature and its inhabitants. Many inventors have been inspired by or simply mimicked these learnings, such as the flying of birds used in designing airplanes and using the shape of dragonflies in building helicopters. Most of the time, social beings (i.e., species that achieve goals through collaboration and cooperation) accomplish tasks without assigned leaders, the same core idea as self-managed teams. Social beings such as ants, bees, wolves, and fish have evolved over millions of years to work together to achieve their goals. The observed behavior of social beings is a potential component of achieving more successful decision-making patterns.

Social beings have similar challenges as humans in self-managed teams. For example, social beings must find ways to improve the quality of their decisions, and they must optimize how they choose and schedule their tasks. Social beings use certain behaviors to overcome challenges in nature such as how bees work together to decide the location of their new nest without anyone playing the role of a leader or when birds follow simple rules to fly together without an assigned dominant bird. These behaviors can indicate better ways to set up self-managed teams and implement successful decision-making processes among team members.

A recent study indicates the success of self-managed teams in the form of teams using Agile models in software development. Agile models provide an iterative, evolutionary approach through the integration of customers and IT team members functioning close to a self-managed team. Although not all Agile teams succeed or represent a full implementation of self-managed teams, they are useful as a starting point for the study of the effective implementation of such teams. Due to recent successful results from Agile teams in IT representing self-managed teams and potential learning opportunities from biomimicry, a study was necessary to understand whether biomimicking the intelligence of social beings can help self-managed team members develop better decision-making approaches in self-managed teams as practiced in IT.

Self-managed teams are organized differently and require alternate implementation approaches from traditional teams such as authorization of responsibilities, clear communication, flat hierarchy, operational freedom, and new coaching roles. Successful self-managed teams may indicate high levels of organizational success; for example, nearly 80% of Fortune 1000 companies implement self-managed teams. Nonetheless, challenges such as groupthink, an unaccepting work culture of employee decisions, and a lack of agreed-upon decision-making approaches, augmented by the absence of managerial supervision, indicate unsuccessful implementation of self-managed teams and the need for specific self-managed team implementation strategies. Corporate leaders in the fast-paced IT industry are increasingly implementing self-managed teams, especially for product development, more than employers in other industries.

When applied to similar problems such as logistics, networks, and optimization in problem-solving, biomimicking approaches, algorithms, and processes have indicated effectiveness. But can we use the similarity of self-managed teams and intelligent swarms to find the right approach for self-managed team implementation and decision-making processes? That is the main question that I will eventually answer in this book, along with approaches to expand what we can learn from biomimicking in leadership and management.

DEFINITIONS

I use certain phrases and terms frequently throughout this book, and surely you have already seen them, so here are some definitions so we can be on the same page:

> *Agile model/method*: Such a model or method is the overarching term for a set of software development methods in accordance with the values and principles stated in the Agile Manifesto.
> *Biomimicking*: Individuals are biomimicking when they imitate the models, systems, and elements of nature to solve complex human problems.
> *Groupthink*: The mode of thinking that persons engage in when concurrence-seeking becomes so dominant in a cohesive ingroup that it tends to override realistic appraisal of alternative courses of action. Groupthink can lead team members to make faulty decisions because of group pressure due to a few members dominating the discussion and disregarding others' ideas (Lee et al., 2016).
> *Intelligent swarm*: An intelligent swarm is a system consisting of many individuals who coordinate activities using decentralized control and self-organization.
> *Self-managed team*: A self-regulated, semiautonomous small group of employees who determine, plan, and manage day-to-day activities and duties under reduced or no supervision is known as a self-managed team.
> *Teamwork*: Teamwork is the process used by team members to work, collaborate, and achieve tasks.

Chapter 3

Standing on the Shoulders of Giants

Sir Isaac Newton once said, "If I have seen further, it is by standing on the shoulders of giants." Newton was, of course, pointing out that he was using the work and knowledge collected and achieved by scientists before him. This book and the research behind it are not an exception. I have relied on the work of many other researchers, especially the field researchers who observe and collect social-being behaviors (Figure 3.1).

So far, we have established that the success of self-managed teams depends on how leaders implement them. Successful implementation of self-managed teams requires organizational transformation strategies. The transformation will need to be structural and cultural to prepare people and organizational structures (like teams and rules of work) for the change. The strategies used by self-managed team members differ from those used by team members in traditional settings with a manager leading the team, so leaders must implement self-managed teams using different approaches. In self-managed teams, members have authority, communicate clearly, and participate actively. Organizational leaders should implement specific strategies for self-managed teams to help team members overcome challenges such as groupthink, which limits some members from participating in team discussions and decision-making. This is the problem we need to solve.

One imaginable solution is to see what we can learn from nature. Scholars and scientists have previously used biomimicking to build and invent many new things. They have also applied some swarm behaviors to formulate new solutions for similar problems in logistics, network, and algorithm optimization. Some researchers have tried to catalog the potential usage of biomimicking and have concluded that it can be used as a sustainable source of innovation in various fields. Researchers who have studied self-managed teams have not focused on an inclusive implementation strategy and instead have focused on writing about general guidance or a limited focus on specific problem areas like leadership, communication, and structure. This indicates a gap in the implementation of self-managed teams and presents an opportunity to evaluate and appraise new self-managed team implementation strategies.

DOI: 10.1201/9781003527206-4

Figure 3.1 Sir Isaac Newton (1643–1727)

Studying the behavior of nonhuman social beings presents a new approach to self-managed team implementation strategies. Many species of social beings, such as ants, bees, and birds, work together on certain activities like finding a nest, fighting intruders, and finding food; without leaders and using simple concepts of swarm intelligence to solve problems, they would be incapable of solving them individually. It is possible to learn from species with social behaviors to improve self-managed teams' implementation and decision-making processes. This chapter includes segments to review various behaviors of social beings, with a summary of patterns at the end of the chapter to summarize what may constitute self-managed team biomimicking behaviors.

The research I did was a multiple case study to present common implementation strategies, such as decision-making processes, experienced by self-managed team members. With the common behaviors of social beings that can be related to teamwork functions in hand, I tried to see if I could find more success, more teamwork and team cohesiveness, and happier team members, where people were acting more like a swarm!

BACKBONE THEORIES

When you look at the sky and see birds flying together and creating mesmerizing patterns and wonder how they do it, you have the first question I had a few years ago. How I ended up connecting the dots between that and team performance improvement is the story of this book (Figure 3.2).

In the search to explain what we can all observe in social beings' behaviors, I looked for established theories in the field. Edward O. Wilson (1929–2021), the inspiring American biologist, presented the sociobiology theory in 1978. Sociobiology is based on evolutionary theory that describes group behaviors and seemingly conflicting altruism displays in nature. In essence, Wilson recognizes social behaviors as part of the evolution of species and explains how group interactions have become part of the biological DNA. As you know, humans also have similar imprints such as a fear of darkness, jumping at the sound of a loud noise, or simply seeking friendships and companionships. Other social beings collaborate or "work together" for direct survival, but complicated human societies can hinder recognizing basic survival needs toward new meanings for success, and so the "work" required to achieve that success may not be recognizable in the form of basic instincts, establishing the need for the science of management and, in this case, more specifically the concepts behind teamwork.

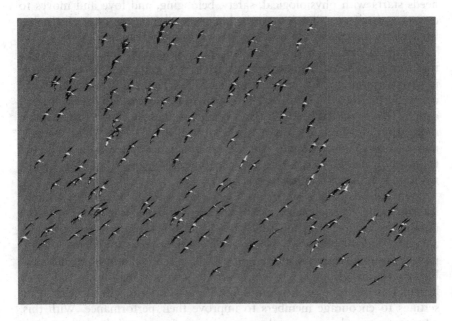

Figure 3.2 A flock of Canadian geese forming a swarm

MOTIVATION

Any effort to bridge successful survival behaviors in nature with human teamwork will require establishing what we know about what motivates us to collaborate with others. One of the theories that is often used to explain motivation to do anything is Self-Determination Theory (SDT). Simple examples include quitting smoking because you value a healthy lifestyle or completing your chores. After all, you value responsibility and delivering the highest-quality work because you care about your reputation. SDT is based on three basic psychological needs.

A prominent researcher in the SDT, Edward Deci, recognized two types of motivation: intrinsic and extrinsic. Intrinsic motivation comes from within, driven by factors that cause individuals to maintain their efforts. Extrinsic motivation comes in the form of rewards presented for completing a task (Deci, 1971). When people are intrinsically motivated, they perform better and achieve higher performance outcomes. This is interesting to us because people working for a company also have a mixture of intrinsic and extrinsic motivations. Extrinsic motivations include salaries, bonuses, awards, and rewards of different shapes and forms. Intrinsic motivation comes from job interest, satisfaction, and passion. Both types of motivation are important in setting up organizations that want to benefit from concepts of self-management.

A well-known model to categorize human needs was first presented by American psychologist Abraham Maslow in his 1943 paper titled "A Theory of Human Motivation." The now-famous Maslow's pyramid of human needs starts with physiological, safety, belonging, and love and moves to esteem and self-actualization. At the highest level of needs, after all else has been satisfied, we want to become what we think we can become.

Recent research on SDT by Deci and his colleague Richard Ryan reveals that out of all possible motivational needs, we seek competence, relatedness, and autonomy the most. According to SDT, humans proactively work on mastering their inner forces, have growth tendencies, and seek optimal actions (Deci and Ryan, 2012). Understanding these needs to foster innate motivation and initiate growth is a critical element of the ability to self-management, a concept that I will explore much more later in the book, but for now, I want you to regard it as a capability to be able to produce results without direct or constant supervision.

In embedded social contexts such as a team setting, intrinsic motivation leads to higher levels of success. With the three pillars of intrinsic motivation (autonomy, competence, and relatedness), autonomous motivation provides a path for individual growth. Hence, if we consider motivation a major component of the success contribution of individuals, and if autonomy and enablement for establishing competency are constructs of that motivation, then leaders must be able to use autonomous motivation in self-managed team settings to encourage members to improve their performance. With this, when team members are ready to participate in teamwork, they improve performance at both the personal and the team level.

WHO NEEDS TEAMS?

You can be one of those people who can do any job perfectly, given time and training. Then you can do anything: build a new car, invent gadgets and devices, and maybe even solve life's biggest mysteries! This would be okay if you had all the time in the world! Human beings discovered the power of many a long time ago. To do a complicated activity, we divide the work between multiple people in the team to achieve the goals more timely and effectively.

There are several reasons for doing the work in a team setting beyond the sheer amount of work. When you work with others, you can benefit from a diverse set of skills, perspectives, and strengths brought in by each team member. Chances of innovation increase. The sense of belonging is a good motivator as the team members can push each other toward getting things done. There will be more learning opportunities as each team member can bring something new to the table. When changes happen, there will be better chances for adaptability and flexibility to process, digest, and deal with the aftermath of the change. The diversity of team members can enhance the chances of problem-solving more efficiently. Even the most individually driven tasks, like breaking a record in individual sports, will be done better when there is a team behind the athlete.

HOW TEAMS WORK?

We use teamwork theory to explain what is needed to use the power of many – the potential power of teamwork. Teamwork theory explains how individuals collaborate effectively to achieve their goals and objectives. There are many components required for successful teamwork, including team dynamics, methods of communication, knowledge, and expertise required and available, and clarity and practicality of goals. There isn't a single model that explains everything, but there are some worth knowing.

Bruce Tuckman's 1965 stages of team development are a good example. There are four (five, if you count a later-added one) stages in the team or group development. These stages have rhyming names that are easy to remember: forming, storming, norming, performing, and adjourning. In the first stage, the team is formed. In most organizations, this is usually done based on what is needed, matching those needs with people who can help with particular aspects of the work. During the forming stage, team members familiarize themselves with each other. The team gets to work, and problems start showing up. In the storming phase, differences cause conflicts. The team members discuss them, fight over them, and "storm" over the available options. Once agreed upon, or forced, the team gets to some "norms" and starts working toward the goals. Team members shape processes in the norming stage, entering the performing stage. When changes happen, or some new issues are discovered, the team members go back as far as the forming stage in some cases to properly bring in more expertise if needed but most likely back to storming to find out what is needed, and new norms are established. After the normalization of teamwork, team members enter the performing stage and start working and getting their job done in an orderly fashion. When there are no major issues, the team is performing, that is, going toward achieving the goals. Once the goals are achieved, the team is dismantled, and work is adjourned.

Another interesting model by Meredith Belbin explores the idea that individuals tend to behave differently and take particular roles within the team. Belbin's Team Role Theory identifies various roles that individuals naturally take within the team. In this model, there are nine roles: coordinator, shaper, plant, monitor/evaluator, team worker, implementer, completer/finisher, resource investigator, and specialist. A coordinator is a person who can imagine the large picture, identify tasks, and guide the team to achieve its goals. Shaper is a team member with competitive tendencies who challenges the team to do better and improve. A plant is a person who brings in creative ideas. Most of the time, they work independently. The monitor/evaluator has an analytical mind and can evaluate situations without bias. A team worker is not exactly a cheerleader but brings a positive atmosphere and helps with team cohesion and conflict resolution. Completer/finisher is detail-oriented and makes sure things are fully done. A resource investigator is someone who likes to explore options and usually has strong connections and knowledge of the outside world. Finally, the specialist is someone with in-depth knowledge and expertise in a particular area. Belbin's theory suggests that we need a healthy balance of these roles in the team to be successful.

The next interesting teamwork model is known as the GRPI model. That abbreviation comes from Goals, Roles, Processes, and Interpersonal relationships. GRPI is a framework developed by Richard Beckhard and David Gleicher and is usually used as a diagnostic model to identify areas of improvement within the team. A team with clear goals, well-defined roles to achieve the goals, the right processes to do the work, and proper interpersonal relationships is set for success.

If you notice, a shared component of all of these models is communication. Suppose the communication is done properly across all team members and during all of the stages of whichever model you consider. In that case, the individuals have a better chance of becoming a team. That collective understanding, which is referred to as the Shared Mental Model, is not easily achieved. Team members should understand the tasks, roles, goals, decision-making process, adaptability to changes, and the right setup for keeping the information flow, or communication lines. To fully understand what really contributes to the Shared Mental Model of the team, we will have to go into the fields of cognitive psychology, cognitive processes, naturalistic decision-making, human factors, and organizational behavior. These are good areas to look into for further reading.

WHO IS GOING TO MAKE IT HAPPEN?

Traditionally, someone with the manager title would control and facilitate achieving goals and objectives for the team. This role in self-managed teams ceases to exist or takes the form of coach or facilitator, at least when it comes to the basic functions and objectives of the team. All the concepts I have provided regarding the teamwork theory apply to all sorts of teams, including self-managed ones. Because self-managed teams do not have assigned managers, team members should receive the proper tools and training to progress through stages of team development and function.

Before I bring in the tools and theories that can help with this aspect of the Intelligent Team, let me review what we already know about the roles of managers and leaders. The study of management and what managers and leaders do requires a whole different book, but for simple differentiation, I will mention the analogy between them: It is said that managers play checkers, but leaders play chess, emphasizing their ability to recognize the value of each person as opposed to focusing on the function being done and asking the same from all the people. Managers use functions and more mechanics of processes, whereas leaders take on the role of support, coach, or facilitator.

So we are naturally more interested in leaders and what they can do for our Intelligent Team. There is already a set of diverse known and discussed leadership styles. These leadership styles vary based on the spectrums of involvement of leaders and followers in making decisions and activities. Max Weber, a socialist, introduced the charismatic leader, who usually takes an *autocratic leadership* role and makes decisions on behalf of the followers. Kurn Lewin, the father of social psychology, is a proponent of *democratic leadership* style. A democratic leader facilitates the discussion to get to an agreed decision.

James Downton and James MacGregor popularized *transformational leadership* by creating motivation and inspiration as the leader's main role. Robert Greenleaf wrote an essay called "The Servant as Leader" and is credited for *servant leadership*, where leaders prioritize the well-being and development of their followers. In the view of Paul Hersey and Kenneth Blanchard, a leader needs to deal with many different situations, so they have to perform *situational leadership* that maximizes the outcome of every case based on the parameters of the situation and available people (Figure 3.3). Finally, to complete the list of leadership styles, we have *laissez-faire leadership*, where the leader takes a hands-off approach, allowing the followers to make decisions and manage their tasks.

There are other leadership styles that do not fit the standard definitions. A particular one is called *shared leadership*, also known as distributed leadership. In shared leadership, the team members share the responsibility of leading based on their skills, expertise, and influence. Collaboration is required from all team members, and decision-making is done through

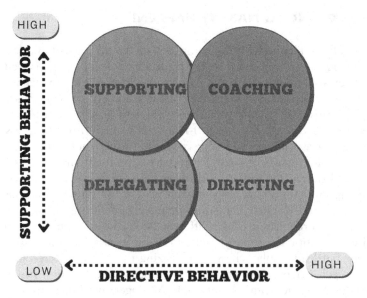

Figure 3.3 Situational leadership based on supportive or directive behaviors

consensus or with input from multiple team members. For shared leadership to be successful, communication should be open and effective. This style may come naturally in managing projects, where experts from each discipline lead different aspects of the project. For example, a project manager leads timelines, tasks, risks, issues, and escalations, among other activities, and a technical engineer takes the technical leadership. In healthcare, nurses, physicians, and other professionals collaborate on a comprehensive plan for their patient care. In education, teachers may collaborate on curriculum, various committees, and school governance. Shared leadership can also be useful in the military, start-ups, and community organizations (Figure 3.4).

For now, have these leadership styles in mind as I continue on the setup for Intelligent Team. I will come back to this topic later in the book.

Considering the leadership styles, two topics stand out: How can the leader be part of the growth of the followers or team members? And how can they set up the team for success, especially when they have to do things more independently? I intend to get these answers from learning from nature, but in terms of existing knowledge and established theories, I will provide a few more relatable examples.

Generally, team members tend to learn from each other. In fact, Albert Bandura's Social Learning Theory, presented in 1977, posits that individuals learn new things like skills and behaviors through their environment; hence, social learning can be as important as direct educational settings. There are three states in the social learning process: observation, imitation, and modeling (Bandura, 1979). So, besides direct education and learning

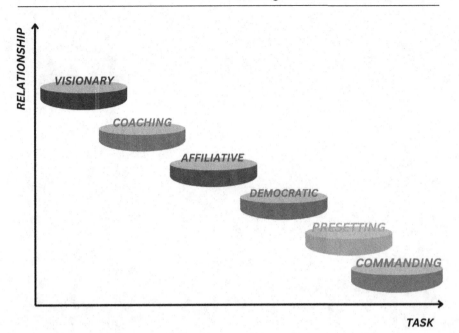

Figure 3.4 Leadership styles based on task and relationship

through direct experience, we tend to observe others, learn what they do through imitation, and model that behavior for ourselves. Leaders may set up the learning process for the followers to receive direct reinforcement of that process. Traditionally, managers administer reinforcements in the form of rewards. The implementation of any successful teams, including self-managed teams, should also provide clear guidance on the contribution and distribution of rewards. Due to a lack of or lesser supervision, there must be alternatives built into any new team models to be used as a driver for measuring success and rewarding hard work. This will be another setup point that I will address later in the book.

Part 2

Self-Managed Teams and Intelligent Swarms

Chapter 4

Self-Managed Teams

When we think of a manager or leader, we think of someone with authority who would make decisions. It would depend on the leadership styles I presented in the chapter before, but all the same, they are the ones making the final call on doing things in a certain way and choosing an option among possible choices. If we want to delegate that responsibility to the team, we need to understand how this delegation may work.

In 1951, Kenneth Arrow presented the social choice theory, which is useful in situations when decisions are to be made involving more than one decision-maker. The social choice theory incorporates the mechanisms for people's participation during decision-making processes. At the core of the theory is a theorem known as the general possibility theorem, which posits that individuals could not make social choices that meet all requirements without options or constitutions that present all possible alternatives (Arrow, 2012). This theorem indicates the drawbacks of voting systems and the complications they can bring to a teamwork setting where decisions may be required frequently. In traditional team management, the manager makes the decisions based on a collection of inputs. Addressing these challenges for any other teamwork setting, including self-managed ones, may require entirely different approaches, which is why I propose a method for learning from nature and mimicking observed nonhuman social being behaviors.

The theory that can connect these challenges with nature and bridge human teamwork with nonhuman social beings is sociobiology theory. Edward Wilson presented sociobiology in 1978, suggesting that evolution could be one way to explain social behaviors. We know that natural selection is the driving force of evolution. Wilson's work in sociobiology shows the benefits of finding similarities and using biomimicking not only in the basic sciences but also in the study of sociology. In the limited view, this society can be teams within a company, and understanding how people interact with one another in a team. This is the core idea of this book, which is based on the proven results of my research, which showed that we can indeed benefit from applying biomimicking and principles of swarm intelligence in group collaboration, running teams, and improving teamwork.

DOI: 10.1201/9781003527206-6

The theories presented in this chapter constitute the framework of this book. Using sociobiology, teamwork, social choice, and other theories elaborated in this chapter, I set out to measure success in teamwork and facilitate productivity in team settings. What I am offering is simple: there seems to be enough evidence to indicate that there are better ways to establish teams that are much more successful, based on the basic principles by which social beings in nature handle their challenges. Somewhere down the road of establishing companies and fabricating rules of conduct for management and workers, we moved away from what we had been doing for eons: learning from nature. Part of this was because it got complicated to truly study groups and colonies in nature, but today, we have enough data collected, enough knowledge collected, and new technologies to learn more about the behaviors of nature and social beings that it is time to see what we might have missed and adopt those methods in our working structures.

This method can provide better opportunities for all the team members to exercise freedom of action and autonomy, be happier in their jobs, become an integrated part of their companies, have a strong feeling of belonging, be more efficient in finding norms, get to perform faster, and make better choices that benefit them and the company as a whole.

Learning and growth are fundamental aspects of teamwork. Social learning theory provides the constructs that team members need to achieve personal growth while completing tasks at the team level. Each team member has a utility function when making decisions or voting. In team decision-making, team members must maximize the aggregation of utility functions. I examined these theories through a sociobiological lens to integrate an understanding of an organic approach for a new team setting – an Intelligent Team.

SELF-MANAGED TEAMS AND BIOMIMICKING

As you read through this book, you'll notice the emphasis on the concept of self-managed teams. This concept is important because the ideal model, the Intelligent Team, needs to be self-managed. In this section, I analyze the self-managed teams with a comparison against traditionally managed teams. I focus on the challenges that members of self-managed teams encounter and compile a list of the potential shortcomings of self-managed teams that members of traditional teams do not face. Then, I examine the approaches in biomimicking and intelligent swarms to show how nonhuman social beings in intelligent swarms solve similar challenges.

Self-Managed Team Overview

By now, you have learned that self-managed team members have much authority to decide how to approach achieving their goals and objectives. Members of the self-managed team receive minimal guidance and influence from outside the team on activities such as planning, organizing, and controlling. Usually, they are provided with a high set of high-level goals and objectives, and they get to decide when and how to approach achieving them. They may or may not be provided with a deadline to achieve the goals, which, of course, is going to influence how they plan for the work.

An important question that you might have is, why do we need to have such teams? After all, isn't having control over the teams within the company better? The answer is no. What we have learned from many research studies around the globe is that if self-managed teams are set up properly (and that is a big if), then they can achieve higher productivity (Parker et al., 2015; Paunova and Lee, 2016). That is why around 80% of the Fortune 1000 companies have integrated self-managed teams into their structures. They may not call it a "self-managed team" either, but the concepts apply, as I will elaborate in the next sections. One common feedback from companies that have gone through the setup of self-managed teams is that the initial thoughts put into the preparation of the team's processes and members matter the most and will define the success or failure of the team. These processes should provide answers to various aspects of teamwork, including work schedules, work methods, supervision, reward systems, and interactions with the rest of the company. I will elaborate on these later in the book.

Why Self-Managed Teams?

As I pointed out earlier, a self-managed team can achieve higher performance; however, to answer the skeptical minds, let's look at some findings from research on this topic. In 2006, Kauffeld identified around ten competency factors and compared them in managed versus self-managed teams. These factors included key performance indicators (KPIs) for success, teamwork effectiveness, cohesiveness, team dynamics, and so on. The results showed a 60% improvement in self-managed teams over the traditional teams. Others have shown that motivation, productivity, and performance of self-managed teams are higher. Members in self-managed generally are more efficient and have a higher sense of belonging, which leads to higher cohesiveness. Other researchers, such as Moe, Dingsøyr, and Dybå, showed that members of self-managed teams "[bring] down decision-making to the level of operational problems and uncertainties and thus increase the speed and accuracy of problem-solving." Team members decide all aspects of work and increase efficiency, cost savings, and productivity, among other benefits. Because self-managed team members have more autonomy and authority, they make better decisions about various work aspects, including approach, roles, responsibilities, and rewards. Accordingly, the teams are more efficient and perform better (Dingsøyr et al., 2016; Dybå et al., 2014; Moe et al., 2008, 2009).

Basics of Self-Management and Levels of Application

The fundamental question is, how do leaders expect to run work through employees without managers? The simple answer is this: Given the right setup, team members can collaborate to address the functions of a traditional manager. The exact approach will differ depending on the implementation of the self-managed team. There are no standards to be followed, as the situations are different. The basic aspects of what needs to be done are not different, but companies do take their own approaches. As elaborated in the following sections, some of the solutions in response to the fundamental question are alternatives such as shared leadership, setting appropriate processes, and/or assigning facilitators.

Let's start with shared leadership. I introduced shared leadership earlier in this chapter.

Shared leadership can enhance team dynamics, foster innovation, and distribute the workload more effectively. However, its success often depends on factors such as trust among team members, effective communication, and a shared commitment to common goals.

At this point, I need to introduce a concept shared between psychology and organizational behavior, called transactive memory systems, introduced by Daniel Wegner in the 1980s. Transactive memory systems refer to methods that groups of individuals use to collectively share, store, retrieve, and distribute information. Team members are aware and have an understanding of who knows what (how the information is encoded in the collective's memory), how it is stored (distributed among the team members), and, when needed, who can present which part of the overall information is needed. Transactive memory systems are used by families, teams, organizations, and social groups.

According to research by Stephanie Solansky in 2008, the effectiveness of shared leadership in self-managed teams leads to a higher level of efficiency and a stronger transactive memory system. Team members use a transactive memory system to perceive, store, and retrieve knowledge. Self-managed team members may be able to use transactive memory systems to reduce the effects of groupthink by establishing more synergy. Members of self-managed teams may not need a single, traditional leader due to multiple shared leaders who provide regular motivational, social, and cognitive support. Leveraging transactive memory systems can contribute to improved collaboration, problem-solving, and overall team performance in various social and organizational settings.

A full measurement of the effectiveness of shared leadership is not easy. For one, shared leadership provides benefits for all types of teams and not just those that are self-managed, making it hard to segregate the effect of shared leadership in association with self-management. Also, informal leadership functions may produce part of the effects observed in team management, leading to inaccurate measurements. Regardless of exact measurement, shared leadership sits on top of transactive memory systems and, with the proper setup for self-management teams, can lead to higher performance.

Up to this point, I have given you indications and tools regarding self-management teams' potential higher performance. To achieve that potential, organizations need to establish a proper structure to support self-management teams, as well as the processes and training required for the team members. These processes should cover all aspects of teamwork, including decision-making, planning, task management, time management, goal management, and reward systems.

Companies may use self-managed teams for many different reasons, including regular work, project work, or driving organizational changes. Three basic principles underlie self-managed teams: (a) assigning team members the responsibility and accountability of taking on and assigning complex tasks; (b) moving from team-member level to team level, allowing team members to set and fine-tune their own processes and assign managerial tasks to themselves; and (c) reaching a balance between organizational and employee interests. The process of building a self-managed team starts with uniting people who eventually form groups, teams, and finally, self-managed teams. Research shows that the presence of a facilitator can lead to more success when performing these organizational and structural changes. The presence of a facilitator or a shared leader can help with the transformation of existing teams into self-managed teams.

In terms of size or industry, the concept of self-managed teams is not limited to large organizations or specific industries. The sense of empowerment and increased performance can be achieved anywhere and with any size. It would just require a proper understanding of roles, interactions, processes, and training accordingly. Research in leaderless self-conducting and traditional singing groups found that all team members felt empowered to take leads and used cues from others for coordination during their performances. This is an open invitation to all teams of all sizes in all industries to set themselves up for higher degrees of success, performance, and enjoyment.

An entire organization can be self-managed, too. The conditions of self-managed organizations differ from the organization of self-managed teams. The approach to a self-managed organization starts with fundamental decisions on the decentralization of authority, levels of self-organization, and application of the required changes. Based on the approach presented by Lee and Edmondson in 2017, employees of certain organizations may have different levels of ability to decentralize work execution, manage and monitor, design organizational and work processes, allocate resources, manage performance, and develop strategy. After employees decide upon the level of self-management, they must establish a formal system to codify the decentralization approach, and then apply the self-management processes organization-wide. Although a few companies have opted to move toward self-management, there are basic gaps and challenges in the required team success levels (Simard and Lapalme, 2019). My basic focus in this will remain at the team level as the building block of a self-managed organization.

How to Build a Successful Self-Managed Team

The transition from a traditional team to a self-managed team requires planning in all aspects, including leadership, authority, and decision-making. For example, the transition of authority may occur in five stages:

1. understanding one-on-one interactions between the manager and the team members,
2. leading interaction to happen between team members by the manager,
3. taking on a coaching role by the manager,
4. team members step up and provide leadership on key team processes, engage others, and
5. leadership reaches its peak level, freeing the manager to attend to higher initiatives than managing the team.

The aforementioned steps show how to reduce the reliance on a particular role and, certainly, also provide a path to prepare team members for a self-managed team state. As traditional team members join self-managed teams, they start taking active ownership roles. Developing and managing knowledge within the team become key contributing success factors. A 1991 research by Watson examined team members' familiarity with each other and the effect of familiarity on group-versus-member problem-solving processes. Findings showed that, as team members gain experience, the influence of more experienced members becomes less essential, a factor directly related to decision-making, groupthink, and inclusion of experience in team decision-making learning exercises. The improvement in decision-making may not immediately appear after setting new processes, enablement, and empowerment, as improvement may take time and effort until team members can provide their true team-added value.

Self-Managed Team Challenges: Leadership

As expected, leadership and decision-making processes differ between self-managed teams and traditionally managed teams. The traditional leadership approach, with a leader making decisions, does not apply to self-managed team members, as it is not easy to set up a functioning team without a leader. The leadership of self-managed teams should stem from four elements: envisioning, organizing, spanning, and socializing. Envisioning and organizing leadership are self-explanatory and common within traditional leadership. Spanning leadership includes activities that occur outside of self-managed teams, within or outside of the organization. In social leadership, similar to shared leadership, multiple leaders take on the tasks of a traditional manager. Social leaders develop and maintain team members' socio-psychological perspectives on concerns, challenges, being heard, and bringing fun and humor to the team.

Although self-managed team members exhibit higher levels of competency and productivity, they also face deficiencies and drawbacks. Establishing self-managed teams takes time, resources, and training. Members of self-managed teams may experience challenges, such as friction between team members and other organizational employees, and have to be able to use preset mechanisms to resolve the conflicts.

Research by Yeatts, Hyten, and Barnes in 1996 compared two self-managed teams, one with members struggling with multiple challenges and the other with members working together smoothly. The researchers concluded that the differentiating factors were team environment, design process, and work process. Decision-making, the most significant advantage of self-managed teams, requires full team involvement with consensus or a majority vote that replaces traditional leader directives. The research confirmed that successful self-managed teams did not have a dominant member in the decision-making process; all members made decisions, with the most knowledgeable person in a particular situation having the most input. Team members should be able to discuss and resolve their differences to reach a consensus or, at a minimum, avoid harboring resentment toward their colleagues. Members of the struggling team took similar approaches, but the supervisor/facilitator tried to dominate the decision-making process. As a result, other team members excluded the supervisor/facilitator, but in the process, they lost his input and his vast expertise.

A year later, in 1997, Wageman examined a similar situation among Xerox employees and compared the success and failure of self-managed teams, leading to the discovery that key success for team members came from effective coaching behavior. Proper coaching provided self-management reinforcement, appropriate problem-solving consultations, and organizational data and information. Poor coaching led to negative outcomes, with team members singled out based on their outcomes, with managerial interventions and overridden team decisions. Wageman compiled a list of activities for traditional leaders and changed the role of leaders to designers, facilitators, and coaches.

The expectation is that employees can work as team members in a self-managed setting, take part in collective responsibility, and self-monitor their performance. To do that, they will need appropriate processes, coaching, and support at different levels of the organization, especially if it is the first time the organization is going through establishing a self-managed team. Due to the involvement of leaders outside the team (at least in the beginning), we do not have exact statistics about the performance of the self-managed teams working their way in new settings, but the research shows that the performance of the team vastly improves if the leadership of the company is in support of the proper establishment of self-managed teams. One hopeful outcome of this book is to provide good information and structure for leaders to negatively affect the performance of the newly established self-managed team.

The leadership of the organization can also heavily influence how individuals perceive their value and role in the success of the team, and because we expect that the members of the self-managed team take on lots of self-responsibilities, this concept becomes even more important. As indicated earlier, team learning is a requirement for a high-performing team, and usually, it starts with the individuals. Learning Goal Orientation (LGO) is a psychological concept related to the attitude of individuals toward learning and success. The focus of LGO is to determine the motivation of individuals in acquiring new knowledge and skills (learning goals) versus demonstrating or validating their capabilities (performance goals). This difference will influence the approach to performing tasks and dealing with challenges.

If learning is the focus, then the team members are intrinsically motivated to learn and find joy in the process, regardless of external awards or validations. Challenges are seen as a part of the learning path, and persistence toward learning is high. However, if the performance goal orientation is the dominant psyche, then the focus is on demonstrating one's competency. External motivations, like rewards and approvals from others, become important. Challenges are avoided to prevent any declines in performance. Perception of success is no longer the journey but the outcomes, and there will be lots of comparisons among peers.

While it's important to have goals in mind, team-learning requires a learning attitude, and the role of leaders to think of providing a learning-oriented balance for the self-managed teams becomes more important than ever.

In 2017, Lee and Paunova researched the effect of LGO on leadership. The researchers proposed and tested this relationship in self-managed team members, concluding that, although a self-learning person feels safer in a self-managed environment and behaves in a leadership role, there are other contributing factors to success. Team members must link LGO and contextual role behavior to achieve the self-organizing goal. In other words, only together social exchange and goal orientation can produce the required leadership outcomes. Team members will not be able to influence team outcomes and performance – even if they have identified goals and use LGO to align with those goals – until they combine their goals with adequate social exchange with the rest of the company or the rest of the world.

Shared leadership is a strong substitute for a traditional leadership role. Self-managed team members can use the shared servant leadership model when and if they need a point of reference or external direction. Team members who take part in servant leadership work toward stronger team behavioral integration. Team members can use servant leadership to promote proper information exchange between team members. The success of the role is measurable through four elements: empowerment, humility, stewardship, and accountability. Research shows a direct correlation between the application of these four measurements and internal and external communication, leading to improved team member performance.

Self-Managed Team Challenges: Non-leadership Aspects

Leadership is not the only challenge that members of self-managed teams must overcome. Self-managed teams need to have counterparts for basic functions similar to traditional teams such as leadership, communication, process improvements, team dynamics, project management, conflict management, consensus decision-making, peer coaching, feedback, group problem-solving, and interpersonal relationships. Self-managed team members must redefine each of these functions as new processes. Please note that I keep on saying "team members" and not "leaders" here because what we have learned so far is that the final steps for setting up the team process should be with the team members so they own it and adjust it as they go.

Giving ownership of the process does not mean that the company does nothing. It is important for organizations to properly establish self-managed teams and give members the necessary training to succeed. Many factors may affect these preparation activities. In addition to leadership challenges, organizational leaders should measure the abilities of team members with an appropriate scale. A solid set of tools for measuring collective efficiency, conflict resolution capability, transactive memory systems (how much team members perceive that each of them possesses team knowledge), and role charts is required. The team designer may not be able to control all the active variables, including team size and team members' familiarity with each other. Additionally, members' different personalities, frames of reference, and values may also affect teamwork. Regardless of these differences, the initial proper team setup with the toolkits mentioned earlier will be key to the team's success.

Due to its importance, I dedicated the last section to leadership and mentioned the possible options that can provide a starting point for functions needed to be covered by the team members in a self-managed setting. Common among all the options is the concept of the collectiveness of the leadership process in such teams. Research has proven that we need to continue the social aspects of team leadership, along with functions like motivation and inspiration. That means we need to make sure that team members continue to interact with the outside world and have systematic methods for motivation and inspiration.

Self-managed team members with experience of cohesiveness and social capital performed efficiently, whereas managed team members who lacked social capital struggled. It is, therefore, necessary to use team members' past experiences (the same characteristics as social capital) as control variables to measure self-managed teams' success. In other words, as we give so much more independence to self-managed team members, we need to replace what we take away, and part of that means relying on the social capital of team members and their past experiences.

Research done by Moe and others has evaluated self-managed team members in different companies and identified team-level and organizational-level barriers. Team-level barriers include personal commitment, team member leadership, and failure to learn; in turn, organizational-level barriers include shared resources, organizational control, and specialist culture (generalists have a range of skills, while specialists focus on specific expertise). As the team relies on these individuals for their contribution, work culture may present a barrier. We can overcome these barriers by cross-training, appropriate team member proximity, appreciation of generalists, establishing trust and commitment, and a one-project-at-a-time rule.

Self-managed team members may also struggle with groupthink. Knowing that self-managed team members are at a higher risk of groupthink, we offer *teamthink* to counter groupthink. With teamthink, a method of thinking within the whole team, team members consider diverse views, openly express or hear ideas and concerns without judgment, recognize team members, and discuss collective doubts.

Although self-managed team members enjoy increased flexibility, they may experience limits and dysfunctions due to conflicts, less personal autonomy, and reduced task interdependencies. There are five types of conflicts: task, relationship, process, inter-sender (requests that conflict with other requests or organizational policies), and resource-related. Although these conflicts are not specific to self-managed team members, they may experience more challenges when attempting to resolve these conflicts independently. In a study of 131 North American companies undergoing organizational change, research showed that self-managed team members are 30% to 50% more productive when these challenges have been explicitly addressed in the self-managed team setup. Researchers also observed that the major obstacle to self-management is the people, and specifically managers. For self-managed team members to succeed, both employees and managers must support the transition to self-managed teams.

Most, if not all, aspects of teamwork have variances in self-managed states. Global teamwork and collaboration are factors that include multicultural perspectives into the combination of success factors. Team members who receive learning orientation overcome multicultural challenges and enable collective global leadership. Other crucial success elements include supporting positive intra-team environments based on trust, safety, and shared identities and advocating strong learning environments. Teams of people with the same cultural backgrounds in major metropolitan areas are rare. Organizational leaders who ignore these differences put teamwork at risk, and more so in a self-managed team setting, as teamwork is more crucial due to differences with traditionally managed teams.

With this, I have pointed out all the aspects of team setup we need. That is all, except maybe the most important one: making decisions. How do self-managed teams decide? That will be the topic of the next chapter.

Chapter 5

Understanding Decisions in Teams

The method of decision-making in self-managed teams is perhaps the most essential factor that differs from traditionally managed teams. In traditional teams, the assigned leader or manager evaluates a situation and makes a decision. Because self-managed team members operate without an assigned leader or manager, they must make decisions differently. In the following sections, I review decisions and decision-making processes and explore gaps in the existing approaches.

DECISION-MAKING IN TEAMS

In the traditional decision-making process, a manager uses prior experience and situational context to decide on the best approach. Given the spatial differences between the design of the classical decision theory and today's complex and dynamic world, there is a need for new decision-making approaches. The technological scene changes faster than in other industries, so decision-making processes that provide the best outcomes can indicate a significant difference in the performance of the team and the company.

The alternative to traditional decision-making is the process of allowing team members to participate. As a concept, this seems fine, although it may overlap with the roles of each team member.

There are two types of roles that the team members will have to fulfill. Activity roles are the team members' core activities. Discourse roles are how team members communicate about their activity roles and how they may influence other activities. The indeterminacy and overlap of these roles within the team's context provide team members with opportunities to contribute to the decision-making process.

The roles mentioned earlier indicate that elements of decision distribution to team members already exist, which self-managed teams can utilize. Team members should be able to contribute to decision-making while acting in their organizational roles. With some rule-setting at the beginning of the teamwork arrangement, it is possible to identify the influence of team

DOI: 10.1201/9781003527206-7

members in their organizational roles with subsequent direction toward the desired direction.

Team members also need access to information and methods of dealing with ambiguity when making decisions as a group. Sometimes, information is not available due to spatial factors, differences in personal approaches to data extraction, cognitive levels, and ambiguity elements. Although the need for structure is an asset when information ambiguity is low, the structure becomes a liability when ambiguity is high. In other words, when the level of unknown elements for decision-making increases, team members can do better if they feel comfortable with less structure in the decision-making process. The need for comfort is applicable in self-managed teams, as the traditional structure of the organization may not be available for decision-making.

Self-managed team members need methods to reach a general agreement or consensus. One proposed model relies on the expert level in a general agreement model to achieve the desired level of consensus. In the traditional model, the decision-maker uses a weighting system, which presents each expert's relevance and importance and, through a feedback mechanism, allows team members to optimize decisions. Members of heterogeneous teams can use the traditional model when experts with different importance and relevance must work together. This model is a notable approach because, in real-life situations, more experienced experts should have higher stakes in each decision, leading to an inclusive and more efficient decision-making model.

Team members must make decisions for different types of tasks, and some decisions may be easier than others. Self-managed team members can use decision-making based on task variety in a model to provide a configurational approach for various team tasks. The target model will need to have a decentralized design but a centralized approach for team coordination. Self-managed team members benefit from guidelines and structure while maintaining authority in a subset of activities where team members are better equipped for coordinated tasks such as decision-making.

The traditional method of decision-making involves investigating the problem at hand, generating options, and weighing them. Let's look at some other models that can help us make faster and better decisions. Each of these models can be applied when a particular aspect of decision-making presents a different challenge or opportunity, for example, time, scope, or people involved. I remember a story about a guy who went to see a psychologist. He told the doctor that it was hard for him to make decisions quickly. The doctor replied that it was normal and that a lot of people are like that. The guy replied, "But I am a football referee!"

There is a decision-making model called Recognition-Primed Decision-making (RPD) developed by Gary Klien. RPD is a model of how people make quick, effective decisions, particularly in complex and dynamic situations. The main contrast between RPD and traditional methods of decision-making is that instead of evaluating all the possible options, RPD allows the decision-makers to rely on past experiences and use the same patterns as in the past. This pattern recognition is sometimes referred to as intuition, but in my mind, a fast internalized analysis is behind what people call intuition. RPD also advocates for a quick simulation of outcomes and continuous parallel processing of information as it becomes available. Finally, RPD doesn't always look for the optimal solution but a "good enough" one. In this way, progress can be made instead of chunks of time being wasted on deciding a perfect solution.

Some of what you are reading might be alarming for people who are used to the traditional model of decision-making, but the concepts of RPD are already used in firefighting, emergency medicine, military operations, and other situations where a fast decision is a must. For these situations, fast decisions are expected and normal, so RPD is simply an adaptation of the mindset into a world of fast-paced changes and opportunities. Members of any team, including a self-managed one, should consider the challenges of traditional models and adopt models they can use to better handle time, change, shifting goals, and uncertainty.

There are no formal steps in RPD, but potential steps (which are not expected to be the same for each group or people) include assessing the situation, identifying recognizable cues, generating options, evaluating the formed decision, making decisions and taking action, and adjusting by monitoring the progress (continuous adaptation).

Another model/theory that can be useful for self-managed teams to make decisions is the social choice theory, briefly introduced earlier in this book. In short, an ideal option to involve all preferences without a perfect rule is extremely hard to achieve. In the absence of that, self-managed team members can use social choice theory's voting mechanisms to resolve situations where preferences among population members cause loops leading to paradoxical states.

There are many aspects to consider regarding social choice theory. For example, does resiliency contribute to decision-making and other social functions? It is proven that resilient team members negate constructive collaboration. The natural inclination to replace a manager's decision-making responsibility is to achieve consensus. Various research shows that team members will struggle to reach absolute consensus or even partial consensus (referred to as soft consensus). This shows we need a well-defined method to reach a decision choice.

SYSTEMS OF DECISION-MAKING

Team members can use established systems such as consensus decision-making, voting-based methods, the Delphi method, participatory contribution (having a say proportional to stake), and dotmocracy (allowing members to use a set number of dots to choose and vote for more important items) to enable the group decision-making process. That process is known as a decision support system (DSS), which can be set up to execute any decision system mentioned earlier. In a DSS, alternatives can be incorporated into the process and followed through the steps until one is selected. Examples of DSS include gatherings (involving everyone), subcommittees, or computer solutions that can facilitate the steps of the process.

Meetings and gatherings are the most basic form of a DSS. I include them as a DSS because they present all the decision-making processes can offer. Of course, there must be a well-defined format for the meeting so that it can run efficiently (which one of us hasn't been in endless meetings deciding on a simple choice?). A few years ago, I was running a key project for one of my clients. There was a decision to be made and agreed upon by the two parties involved. On the date when a meeting was scheduled to happen to make the decision, I had to deal with some other emergencies, so I couldn't attend. I tried to make it very simple and arranged the decision to be a yes/no question. The day after the meeting, my colleague told me they decided on "yes," but when I was talking to the partner company person about how to execute the "yes" decision's post-actions, he was surprised because he thought they had agreed on the "no" decision! This example shows how different the perceptions of a discussion can vary and demonstrates the clear structure and checkpoints required. You can have meetings and gatherings, but if you don't have a clear understanding of what the choices are, how to lead the discussion, how to ensure that everyone is properly providing feedback, and, finally, make a decision that everyone understands, Murphy's law will absolutely apply!

If the scope of the decision is wide, then you may need to establish subcommittees or subgroups to come up with decisions or background information related to each particular area. Each subgroup will act as a new team and collect information. Then, when needed, the subgroup provides decisions or a summary of information needed for the decision in the original team. This concept will be discussed later on.

Then, we have automated DSSs, which are computerized systems that help with the decision-making process by providing data in various reports, comparative and historical views, and, in some cases, cross-company information. The leaders will assess the DSS system data to make decisions. However, very few provide tools for managing the process itself, and none provide solutions for self-managed teams.

Regardless of using an automated system or more traditional ways to discuss and make a decision, there are well-known systems and approaches for making a decision when multiple people have to contribute. I explore these systems and approaches in the subsequent sections.

Getting to a Consensus

In consensus decision-making, group members help and participate in finding a decision that best supports the group members' overall interests. As the term *consensus* indicates, unless otherwise specified, everyone should agree with the selected option and the decision. The decision should be unanimous, as observed in the jury decisions in the North American court-room system.

Challenges arise quickly, though: What if some members do not agree with the resulting outcome? A quick solution can be changing the setting from unanimous agreement to a near-unanimous agreement or full consent. Remember, one of the principles of self-management is the participation of everyone, so we do want to find ways to keep everyone's ideas in the decision pool. There are other options, such as applying shades of agreement and using fuzzy logic, but they are not widely available and are too complex.

The simpler options include unanimous agreement minus one or two votes, Condorcet consensus or voting (voting on a preference/priority basis), a supermajority (with set thresholds such as 90%, 75%, or 60%), a simple majority, or escalation of the decision to a committee or leadership. These are all self-explanatory except for Condorcet's consensus. Marquis de Condorcet was an 18th-century philosopher and mathematician. Condorcet voting is a method to determine the winner among the candidates based on pair comparisons between candidates. A candidate who could beat all others in pair comparison would be the winner.

The team may choose to use any of these methods as the general approach or decide to choose one for a particular decision. Whichever method or approach, though, the basic requirements for getting to a decision are sharing information, active listening, discussing options, and allowing everyone to be heard. The "difference" between the points of view can be resolved through discussions. The problem that everyone should avoid is the "indifference" of members. Success in our desired team setting requires the participation of everyone.

Another principle worth mentioning is the de-association of names from solutions or ideas. A team member can indeed bring in a brilliant solution, but for a team to be successful, that solution is the team's, and branding it with the initial owner of the idea alienates others. In reality, because in teamwork everyone is familiar with their own aspect of work, through team discussions and participation of others, the original ideas will evolve and improve. If it is branded under a person's name, others may naturally hold back from contributing, which is a loss in true teamwork toward an Intelligent Team.

When discussions start on options and ideas, objecting members to a particular idea should contribute their concerns, which may be a blocking issue that removes that option from the pool of decisions or simply becomes a drawback in the list of disadvantages for the option. All of these are decided by the team through the agreed-upon methods mentioned earlier.

These discussions can be in an open form, but preferably a step-by-step process can improve the performance of the team to get to the decision.

Through the experience, the team members will eventually follow the steps automatically, but to begin with, they should

1. frame the topic,
2. have open discussion,
3. identify concerns,
4. collaborate on building the best proposal or option,
5. select the best option and set the direction, and
6. synthesize towards implementing the option.

Another aspect worth mentioning here is emotion. Human beings are emotional. In response to external events, we tend to display various emotions, including enthusiasm, anger, or detachment. During the process of implementing any change, the organization's leaders ought to keep emotions in mind, and implementing a new method of arranging members into teams and running a self-managed team is not an exception. In fact, similar to groupthink, the probability of an extra display of emotion is higher, simply due to the fact that it may remain unchecked, especially if the emotions materialize in the form of detachment and indifference in team members.

Acknowledging that, we need to bake the tool of dealing with emotions into the tools and structures we build for the self-managed teams toward our Intelligent Team. These tools can be personal and/or team-level methods of dealing with emotions directly or indirectly. In this way, the role of the organizational leaders changes from decision-makers to decision architects. As such, they may be able to address emotions indirectly by a structured team design that controls the emotions through the process to instigate the right emotions and biases (indirectly), or they may have a process that deals with emotions directly (facilitators in discussions, etc.), simplifying the processes, or official increased accountability.

Group Decision-Making Facilitators and Challengers

In the next few sections, I intend to bring up aspects of working within a group/team setting that can be facilitators or challengers in making decisions. I hope this awareness allows organizational leaders to be mindful of what may work for or against their design for the team, but the general proposal for Intelligent Team will also deal with these directly or indirectly.

Groupthink

Groupthink is a situation that occurs when subgroups of team members drive team decisions that may not include all courses of action. Team members may struggle with groupthink, leading to a weakening of the chance of establishing cohesion. The occurrence of groupthink can be a significant drawback of self-managed teams. In self-managed teams, the lack of a designated central leader often causes smaller groups of members within the team to use their experience, influence, or personal agendas to overestimate, underestimate, and maintain closed-mindedness. Generally, structural issues within the team, situational context, and high cohesiveness within sub-teams cause groupthink. Lack of team structures and potency can also lead to groupthink. Team members who engage in groupthink negatively affect team cohesion and members' well-being, as that is one of the reasons why indifference and, eventually, detachment from the team ignites. Because self-managed team members may be prone to groupthink, they should be equipped with strategies to avoid groupthink in the team setup. Each team member can help avoid groupthink if they are able to object to proposed decisions. In fact, participation should be encouraged and, to some degree, become a must until it becomes a fabric of every team member's mindset. Suppose there are higher-ranking individuals as part of the team. In that case, they should either avoid voicing opinions or wait until everyone has opined and, even then, emphasize that they are just one of the team members and that all the alternatives should be evaluated equally. The leaders' and higher-ranking members' participation is one of those candidate cases for Delphi methods where voting is done in secret. For each solution, a designated opposing member should challenge the solution, offering improvement by proposing further adjustments. Team members should reconcile their different perspectives through negotiation, clarifying questions, and asking for details and supporting documents and evidence.

Usually, team managers are responsible for providing such an environment. In the case of a self-managed team, addressing groupthink will present as a gap that the team setup and collaboration process should take care of.

Whereas the dominance of a few members through groupthink may have negative effects, team members who overanalyze also present drawbacks. Recent research in the U.S. government on decision-making processes found significant delays in decisions due to overanalysis. In accordance with rigorous existing system processes, decisions follow vigilant decision-making. The research showed that subcabinet executives dealt with latencies caused by overanalysis. A balance is needed between dominating team members quickly deciding what to do and everyone's potential indifference or overanalysis.

The process that I will derive not only should help team members resolve groupthink but also needs to be able to deal with the problem of overanalyzing team members. Part of that approach will be to train members for decisiveness and a preference for action to improve their performance from good to great.

Due to the advancements in technology and the encouragement of online communities emboldened by pandemics, team members of many organizations can function virtually. Groupthink may appear or occur differently in online communities. Research shows the antecedents of groupthink, including cohesion, structural faults, and provocative situations, can be indicative of the existence or growth of groupthink. It seems virtual team members tend to overestimate their work to protect their subgroup. Structural changes and provocative situations in the research of online team members indicated closed-mindedness, another symptom of groupthink.

Self-managed team members may amplify the effects of groupthink due to team design. In other words, the team design or team setup can encourage groupthink. As such, given the new team design that I am proposing, it becomes even more important that methods of groupthink avoidance be integrated into the change processes to establish an Intelligent Team.

What are the elements that need to be included in the process? Here is a good list to start with:

1. Environment: Overall parameters that define our working relationships, including team members' experience in the company or in the past, the atmosphere of team discussions, and empowerment from the leaders of the company. If the team members were asked if they feel empowered to truly participate in team activities without prejudgment, how would they answer?
2. Decision-making process: This will be a centerpiece for the Intelligent Team design and will be discussed in detail later in the book, but obviously, through the process, we will enable/require the participation of team members in the decision-making process, which will help with the groupthink/overanalysis problems.
3. Facilitation: The new team design should still make team members feel they are supported and that they can ask for it when needed, which may come in the form of facilitation by a designated person (who is not a member of the team, so they are not influencing anything) or can be a rotation of team members.
4. Education: Part of the new team design/setup will be creating awareness of many new ways of doing teams, and education and awareness regarding groupthink will be part of it.
5. Full team involvement: I have mentioned and emphasized this so far already, but it is one of the most important constructs of groupthink avoidance.

All of these elements are present even if the team design is in the traditional setting of having a manager, but they get fully augmented in self-managed teams. So the setup and its associated processes should enable the team to watch for and control groupthink.

Group Decision-Making Synergy

Self-managed team members need to find successful decision-making approaches. A factor of team decision-making is members' ability to use team *synergy* to make more effective decisions than those made by each team member individually. In that way, self-managed decisions based on proper processes are better than decisions made by one person or a manager. In organizational terms, synergy occurs when members work together as a group and outperform individual members. In the absence of dedicated leaders, a positive team synergy indicates success that will be reflected in many aspects of teamwork, specifically in decision-making.

Some factors may work against the synergy in the team. One of these factors is allowing personal biases into the decision-making processes. Personal biases exist, so all we can do is ensure that they do not get into the teamwork. The best tool to help with this is communication, through which team members share information about their backgrounds and desired outcomes from the decision or group activity. Biases are usually hidden until the right questions and communication bring them out. Once the existence of a bias is recognized, the awareness itself is a major tool to try to keep it out of work.

Another factor in a team's synergy is stakeholder involvement and strategic alignment. If the organizational leaders can provide a good overall strategy, explain why that strategy is important, and involve the stakeholders directly in it, it leads to better synergy. The effects of the cascading strategy show the significance of proper guidance for all employees, especially self-managed team members, as they require strategic guidance to make decisions with minimal supervision.

How can we increase and protect the team's synergy?

1. **Clear Communication:** Both of the factors mentioned earlier can be dealt with through clear and open communication. Being on the same page helps avoid many issues while creating a higher level of team synergy.
2. **Define Roles and Responsibilities:** Once the goals are clear and people are not a mystery to one another, it also has to be clear what each team member is expected to do. Roles and responsibilities may be different from one project to another. In fact, it is a well-known project management practice to review roles and responsibilities at the beginning of each project to make sure everyone is clear about their share of the work. This is directly transferred to a self-managed team setup. Clarity around the roles and responsibilities saves time in the long run and provides a means of working together efficiently. Clearly define the roles and responsibilities of each team member. When everyone knows their specific contributions, it helps to avoid confusion and ensures that tasks are completed efficiently.
3. **Promote a Positive Team Culture:** Perhaps a prerequisite to all team setups is establishing a positive and supportive team culture. Only then will the team members feel comfortable and safe to share their ideas, question ideas from others, and truly participate in team activities, including decision-making, leading to better collaboration.

4. **Team Building Activities:** I usually run various team-building activities in my classes to show the students how real teams are formed and how work is normalized during heated conversations. Team-building activities, no matter how simple, have an immediate effect on establishing team synergy and the start of work relationships and trust among team members.

5. **Utilize Technology:** The availability of information and the ability to process them is a key to success in making better decisions. With recent technological advancements and the boom in the amount of information available, there are many distractions. Research shows that applying the principles of self-managed teams can provide the focus that the team needs. To support that, we need to have proper collaboration tools and technology that facilitate communication and information sharing. This includes project management tools, messaging apps, and video conferencing platforms.

6. **Set Common Goals:** This is the same principle I mentioned earlier. Providing a common picture and involving the real stakeholders is key to establishing the synergy within the team.

As the team's synergy scale goes up, the team members establish and elevate what is known as team cohesion – the emotional connection – and support that team members exhibit toward each other. I will elaborate in the next section.

Cohesion

Group cohesion is a critical factor for successful synergy. As group cohesion increases, interactions and communication levels go up. Team members with cohesion collaborate and coordinate to a higher degree. A team model should provide tools to increase cohesion. Used as a measure of team success, cohesion may be apparent in both personal psychology and team psychology.

For self-managed teams, cohesion is even more important. With increased team cohesion, team members can achieve better results, especially in decision-making. One way to increase cohesion is to have traditions within the team. Start the day with a team huddle as they do in sports, or ring a bell when a milestone is achieved. These rituals, no matter how simple, establish a sense of belonging. In a start-up company long ago, we maintained a cardboard thermometer, with the number of assets we managed as the measure of success. The midstream and ultimate goals were marked on it, and every time we hit one of those, the team would celebrate. In 2016, Watson-Jones and Legare posited that one of the benefits of team ritual – practiced behavior – is increasing social cohesion. Teams that engage in rituals with a positive view affect cohesion and decrease conflicts. Rituals may include work procedures and nonwork activities such as dining, gaming, and social events, in which team members can participate to increase team cohesion.

Factors influencing team cohesion are quite similar to elements contributing to a team's synergy, including having common goals, sharing the same interests, and striving for member satisfaction. As usual, for the purpose of this book, to find the proper setup for Intelligent Teams, we should integrate these factors. An element to watch for is leadership. Authentic leadership has a positive effect on team cohesion and identification. If team members identify as part of the team, they start to care about each other, leading to higher levels of cohesion. Team members who use authentic leadership promote positive psychological awareness and positive ethical environments, transparency, balanced information processing, and cultural awareness. Authentic leadership is another element that self-managed team members can apply to the design of their teams.

Two issues have negative effects on cohesion: polarization and groupthink. An outlet of polarization, referred to as the risky shift phenomenon, occurs as team members take higher risks when making decisions within team settings than when making the same decisions alone. We want the team members to feel better about the team and the support that they can receive from others, but just because there are many people on the team, the risks of the work do not go away, and an adequate amount of due diligence still needs to take place. Team members may experience counterproductive polarization when group members' initial consensus becomes extreme or when members ignore facts in favor of the initial verdict. The process of avoiding polarization requires managerial support and proper setup in a self-managed team setting, which is a current gap we will address in our Intelligent Team model.

To address the risky shift phenomenon, we simply need to train the team members to follow the process and set reminders at each point of decision-making that everyone asks all the right questions. If anyone has a concern, their input should be fully considered. If all of the members are considering the same option, then maybe they can designate someone from the team, or even an expert from outside the team, to play devil's advocate and question the solution.

Research shows that the likelihood of polarization occurring is when the goals of the team members are not aligned with the goals of the overall team. If this is observed at the time of team setup, then we can adjust the processes and, as a result, the outcomes accordingly. The occurrence of groupthink is a by-product of polarization, as influential individuals may directly or indirectly persuade others to follow them in group decisions. This happens even if the goal of those members is simply to get noticed, or in more complicated situations, if their goals include other things such as promotions.

Group polarization is one of the main challenges to team performance. Team members need cohesion to improve decision-making, and polarization has a negative effect on decision-making. Polarization is a demonstrated behavior in court and jury members' decision-making process. That's why there is a rigorous process in jury selection, as the only goal will need to be judging based on information, without any biases, and getting to a consensus in due time, and not due to any other reasons. In the case of a self-managed team, members may experience augmented effects of polarization due to a lack of direct supervision, which will need to become part of the fabric of team setup and processes.

When group polarization and pressure to conform occur, team members may struggle to make decisions due to escalating tendencies and the inclination to expend more resources to justify previously used resources. Resources may be the money or time dedicated to a previous commitment and could be as implicit as the time spent in meetings to explain previous decisions. When polarization occurs, team members or smaller groups of members within the team spend part of their time and energy to further their investments in areas that do not merit additional resources. Managers track polarization patterns as risks. Leaders setting up self-managed teams should establish a process to check risk patterns and provide corrective guidance, thus dealing with polarization through initial team setup and then followed by processes during decision-making.

Self-managed team members can mitigate the risk of decision-making polarization by using deliberative norms. Deliberative norms are simple rules that members communicate and facilitate within the team. To reduce group polarization, self-managed team members can use deliberative norms to provide opportunities for discussions instead of arguments. When team members exchange ideas, they can express thoughts and opinions, have the right discussions, and foster true alignment without polarization to make decisions. In some sense, the root of polarization is the sunk cost of the project, which, as finance people know very well, should not be part of the decision-making process and should not weigh anything unless in alignment with goals at its current state.

Decision-Making in Self-Managed Teams

The transfer of authority from leaders to team members differentiates self-managed teams from traditional teams. This difference is noticeable in decision-making events. In an organizational hierarchy accepted by team members, the quality of decisions, the support of decisions, and, as such, the performance is high. The psychological safety of team members' buy-in provides opportunities for teams to overcome autocratic behaviors like groupthink. In self-managed teams, however, this process does not work. In self-managed teams, therefore, team members should replace managers' roles with processes as a part of the team setting. One of the team members in each case may assume the role of facilitator to execute the process, preferably in a rotation or even bringing a facilitator when needed. With the right setting and execution of the decision-making processes, self-managed team members make more effective decisions because they know the job better than anyone else.

How can self-managed team members make better decisions? Recent research discovered that if the team members shared a mental state, the effectiveness of the team and decision-making outputs increased. Team members can share a mental state when they receive appropriate, adequate information and facilitate discussions before decision-making, something that is part of the nature of self-managed teams.

Also, it is reported that team members equipped with action processes made successful decisions. Action processes include formulation review, coordination, and decision revisiting. Team members who follow action processes improve performance when they review, discuss, and revisit team decisions.

Self-managed team members should refine the decision-making process in their team setting so they can make better, more inclusive decisions to reach a consensus. Because they share both decisions and consequences, team members can implement shared decision-making by studying the consequences of different levels within the organization. This model provides opportunities for team members to participate in the decision-making process, as they are directly accountable for the consequences.

Organizational leaders may use self-managed teams to foster participation among all members because whole-team participation leads to better performance for processes such as decision-making. The traditional models of team management and decision-making include managers who perform these tasks.

The last couple of chapters showed underlying factors in making decisions within the team and issues that may arise specifically in a self-managed team setting. We are now ready to explore nature and see what it might be able to offer.

Chapter 6

Intelligent Swarms

It's finally time to see how intelligent swarms can help us build Intelligent Teams. For that, we will start from the simplest forms of self-organization and build from there. These days, we hear more and more about our creations doing things on their own, doing self-checks, performing self-analysis, software with self-healing code, and, of course, the recent boom of AI, machine learning (ML), and new horizons that apparently have scared some people (*technophobia* is the term).

Let us recognize that self-organization, in its most basic form, is a phenomenon that occurs when simple rules produce complex patterns. This can be observed from atomic levels up to complicated human societies. Carbon atoms, pressured and heated together, align to create diamonds. In a crystal, atoms align in specific ways. Those crystals then form patterns in seashells. The complex structure of the seashell began with atom formation in crystal patterns that led to a much larger structure. In this case, the primary forces are the simple rules of force between atoms. In biology, simple rules of chemistry and physics allow the cells to function. Birds fly together, and fish swim together to avoid their natural predators. They each follow some simple rules. There is no leader, but the end result, from a bystander's point of view, is as if they are all one entity led by a higher form of intelligence. The premise of self-organization is the same, as there is no central director other than simple rules. The higher level of intelligence is a manifestation of hundreds or thousands of members following the same rules, demonstrating an intelligent swarm.

For a team to become a self-organizing entity, team members should respond collectively to internal and external changes, thus becoming a complex adaptive system. Members of this adaptive system show intelligence when they collectively react to changes in smart and appropriate ways. Swarm intelligence is an emergent property of teams that enables members to resolve challenges and problems in ways that would not otherwise be possible at team-member levels.

In 2009, Miller and Page proposed eight criteria for collective adaptability to occur. These criteria are loosely based on Buddhism's path. The eightfold path includes right view (the ability to receive and understand others), right

DOI: 10.1201/9781003527206-8

intention (a common goal that they all want to achieve), right speech (the ability to send and receive information), right action (the ability to influence others by doing something), right livelihood (a rewarding system; the reason for participation), right effort (strategies to work and function with others), right mindfulness (the same or similar rationality), and right concentration (the ability to focus on the event or the task with the highest priority). Each of these can apply to different levels of life-forms; for example, humans use language and body gestures to communicate, and cells in the human body use chemical substances to send messages. Wrong chemicals or wrong words do not work.

Social beings (including many species of animals and insects) generally follow simple swarm intelligence rules as if they are working together or being led by a leader or an entity with a different level of intelligence. For example, each fish in a school moves in the same direction as other nearby fish, maintains a distance from neighbors, and changes direction and follows neighbors when other fish alter their path. Fish use these rules to escape from danger and move toward food or a better location.

Of course, members of the team will need more complex processes than just moving together, but the underlying idea is the same. For example, if team members can follow simple rules to lean toward one of the options in a decision-making process, the movement of schools of fish is not far from a decision-making model. This concept has proof in mathematics that indicates that in responding to questions with definitive answers, the group members as a collective always outperform individuals. The concept is called diversity prediction theory, which indicates that collective error is equal to the average participating person error minus prediction diversity. Therefore, decisions made or actions taken by collective group members always provide better results with higher diversity.

We can observe the effects of using simple rules in decision-making in more complex societies. For example, when a herd of baboons needs to use a path of moving, they use a simple voting system. The few dominant herd members show a willingness to go in different directions, especially if the degree of disagreement is high. They wait for the herd members to decide the direction by showing support for each of the dominant herd members' selected paths. They stand closer to the path they prefer to generate a demo-cratic collective action. Once decided by the majority (I don't think they count exact numbers!), the herd moves in that selected path.

Group decisions have received centuries of study. Marquis De Condorcet published *Application of Analysis to the Probability of Majority Decisions* in 1785, in which he set forth what is known as Condorcet's jury theorem. In this theorem, Condorcet theorizes that the quality of the decision-making process does not necessarily improve with the number of voters. The probability that each voter will decide correctly indicates the quality of the decision-making process. If this probability is less than 50%, increasing the number of voters may cause a wrong decision. This is the simplest version of the main theorem, as researchers have presented many varieties and applications of Condorcet's theorem.

We need rules that team members can use to improve decision-making processes and teamwork. These rules should include approaches for dealing with groupthink, decision-making alternatives, team-wide inclusion, and choosing pragmatism over idealism. For example, members can avoid groupthink by stepping away from the situation to think individually. Also, team members can plan for emergencies so that making rapid decisions becomes simpler due to what team members have already discussed about boundaries, priorities, timing, and exit rules.

To foster alignment and stronger decision-making, team members need to equally allocate resources to alternative decisions; investigate alternatives thoroughly before dismissing them; present issues to all team members; study how members of more successful teams approach tasks; and, once ready to decide or vote, choose the most practical method over the ideal method. These simple rules, once properly set up as team processes, can provide guidance at the team-member level for improved teamwork and quality decisions.

The concept of learning from the natural models and mimicking them is not new. The core purpose of this book is to present how social beings work together and demonstrate group-level intelligence and then apply the proven methods and behaviors in team activities, including the most challenging ones, like decision-making.

By definition, swarm intelligence is the collective behavior of decentralized and self-organized swarms. Many organisms, including insects and animals, collaborate to accomplish larger goals and objectives. Each member of the group follows simple rules perfected over millions of years of evolution.

There are similarities between the activities and goals of these swarms and a team and its members. In intelligent swarms, members lack designated leaders. All swarm members are equal, and they work together to solve a wide array of challenges, something well researched in mathematics and computational models. Researchers have applied swarm intelligence to a range of problems, including finding optimized solutions, applying probability distributions, dealing with different numbers of behaviors, exploiting the positional distribution of agents, coping with a variety of control parameters, managing the generation of new agents, using the concept of velocity in optimization, and utilizing different types of exploitation. During my research, I mapped each of the listed behaviors to one or more aspects of self-managed teams.

Examining the applications mentioned indicates the value of how swarm intelligence simulation presents different approaches for various team functions such as decision-making. Mimicking intelligent swarms increases team members' performance and output. Self-managed team members can apply swarm intelligence when establishing approaches for team functions and decision-making processes through the processes and tools provided by this book. Table 6.1 shows how teams can apply swarm intelligence to areas of interest, as well as opportunities to enhance or improve team performance

Table 6.1 Comparison of intelligent swarm behaviors with self-managed implementation strategy

Intelligent swarm behavior	Self-managed team implementation strategy
Following an optimized solution to the problem	• Strategy selection • Find different methods for solving problems • Decision-making process • Progress update
Applying probability distributions	• Decision Approach
Dealing with different numbers of behaviors used	• Dealing with personalities • Team norms and culture
Exploiting the positional distribution of agents	• Using expertise • Training team members to get closer to each other
Dealing with a variety of control parameters	• Dealing with the complexity of models
Managing the generation of new agents	• Onboarding members • New hires
Using the concept of velocity in optimization	• Coordination between the members of the team
Utilizing different types of exploitation	• Market/external input/finding

or outcomes. These areas underwent exploration and mapping as implementation strategies for self-managed teams in the following sections. Do not worry about what exactly the table means yet; everything will be explained and clarified throughout this chapter.

UTILIZING INTELLIGENT SWARMS

Many interdisciplinary studies have presented data on intelligent swarms, with each study expanding on one or a few bio-inspired processes or algorithms. Bats, fish, fireflies, cuckoos, bee colonies, wolves, and many other social beings collaborate to achieve complex goals. These social beings act in groups, swarms, or colonies that exhibit forms of intelligence at large.

The hard work is done by the biologists who conduct field studies of intelligent swarm behaviors in long-term research studies, expedited with new findings made possible using the latest technologies, such as video analysis. Most likely, a lot more is to come with all the AI tools that are becoming readily available on a daily basis. Applied researchers use these findings in various forms, sometimes in simplified models that scholars in various fields can utilize. For example, a simple model of schools of fish, known as the artificial fish swarm algorithm (AFSA), is used to model a dispatching method for taxis. In another case, the behavior of bee colonies was applied to a variety of applications to find the optimum solution and performance increase. In the following sections, I will present such findings to articulate areas correlating with the application of intelligent swarms in self-managed teams toward building the right setup for Intelligent Teams.

Learning From Bats

Bats apply short signals in a method known as echolocation, their ability to use variable frequencies to find objects and prey. Through this signal, bats can measure distance, the target's orientation, the type of prey, and its speed. The complete logic and processes used by bats are extremely complicated. For that reason, researchers have simplified the behavior into algorithms. There is a simple algorithm for bats that includes echolocation and usage of frequency, pulse emission rate, loudness, amplitude, and pulse rate to control parameters and adjust to the optimum positions. In accordance with this algorithm, the movement of a bat becomes a series of position adjustments toward its prey based on echolocation parameters until it achieves its goal. This algorithm is a continuous one; that is, each adjustment comes as a very close point comparing the last one in the virtual bat's decision system to change its direction or keep the course. Later, others optimized the bat algorithm for a discrete version to apply in situations when a constant or continuous survey of positions is not possible or cost-effective.

This research is interesting in relation to decision-making processes, in that it allows for a variety of selection processes of permutations. In the proposed algorithm, the moving agent (bat) uses simple methods of swapping (between two possible new positions) and crossover to find the optimum solution by updating the direction, the velocity of movement, and the overall position of the goal.

Variations of bat algorithms are modeled for different situations, thus necessitating exploration to find optimum versions for self-managed team applications. Bats continuously seek the environment and adjust their courses based on updated locations of prey and other bats. The main differences between these variations are the frequency of the external checks and the periodic adjustments instead of the continuous natural model. One variation to note is the binary bat algorithm, proposed for improving feature selection. In this variation, which is used to optimize search frequency, bats use binary mechanisms to choose their next best positions.

In relation to self-managed teams' setup, we can apply bats' approaches to moving toward their goals in their decision-making processes. Bats live in large groups and use the same simple rules to move around and toward their prey. In a self-managed team, each person should evaluate the choice between options (and, if possible, a binary selection between only two options as it's easier to discuss and compare two). As all team members evaluate choices, they find the preferred option and approach a decision. Bats continuously use their method, but team members can discuss at intervals as they collect more information and move toward ideas presented by others; individuals can then consider the final results to make the decision.

Particle Swarm Optimization (PSO) is a similar biomimicking pattern, presented as a simple algorithm that provides a method for simulating social behaviors. Inspired by the synchronous and choreographed moves of flocks of birds, particle swarm optimization searches for each bird's rules of movement. These rules allow birds to fly in mesmerizing coordination. In mapping the physical world to the social experience perspective, some of the boundaries of the cognitive or experimental variables merit reconsideration. For our purposes, physical movement is similar to bat movements, that is, having the goal in mind and making corrective actions to keep on moving toward the target. Also, we can use these similarities to map the beliefs and attitudes of our peers. The proposed particle swarm optimization presents the concept of "collision" differently from the physical world; two birds cannot occupy the same physical space, but people with different beliefs can. Hence, despite the negative intonation, in using these algorithms for aligning, we actually want the collisions to happen when it comes to people's thoughts and emotions. Also, particle swarm optimization presents the velocity of agents in swarms (team members reach a certain understanding at their own pace) as well as a stochastic variable (to provide reasons for randomness observed in social behavior) for faster approaches and better solutions.

To summarize the takeaways from the bat algorithm, binary bat algorithm, and particle swarm optimization, self-managed team members should receive as much information as possible so they can evaluate various options. Team members must receive encouragement to build their knowledge and take smaller steps to approach decisions, which indicates the realities of changing goals in business and the work environment and the constant motion of ultimate goals. Team members can see how others in similar positions moved forward. The key bat and bird biomimicking patterns include incremental knowledge-gaining, consultation with nearby team members, iterative evaluation of overall goals, and validation of the direction of thoughts and decision-making points. I included these elements in my research and have applied them in the model I will present for Intelligent Team in later chapters of the book.

Learning From Fish Swarms

Certain species of fish move together for food and protection. The large number in the school of fish scares away predators and allows the fish to eat while others create an image of a large creature. As in other swarms, fish do not have leaders, yet they act and work together as a unit. While the swarm may seem very complicated, the movements are established by simple rules again: move in the same direction, keep a close distance from others around, and go for a bite if food is close.

As indicated earlier, the fish behavior is already simplified in the AFSA algorithm. AFSA is a population-based evolutionary computing technique that uses the social behaviors of fish in schools. The simplified version of AFSA provides easy rules/actions that each fish uses, including search, swarm, chase, and leap. Each of these can turn into a function in the algorithm, in that each agent in the swarm searches around to see who/what is close by, simply "swarms" by swimming according to the direction of the swarm, chases the food, and leaps toward the location required.

The main input element in this behavior is the scope of vision of every fish. If the vision is empty, the fish can do a random search and move to a new position. If the vision is crowded, the fish moves in a direction based on the positions of other fish in the vision. If the vision is neither empty nor crowded, the fish can swarm or chase a better position. In the swarm state, the direction is based on visible fish positions, and in the chasing state, fish search for the best position toward their desired directions.

AFSA presents an essential aspect of swarm intelligence application to the improvement of self-managed team members: different behavior based on the scope of vision. In other words, we have members of the team who see different aspects of the same problem and/or know more or less about a topic or situation. These differences, if not considered and baked into the process, will become sources of anxiety, groupthink, and disengagement.

AFSA has already been used in many practical applications, such as optimizing job scheduling in grid computing. For the purpose of improving Intelligent Team design, we can apply the concepts of visual fields to physical and cognitive teamwork, presenting cognitive visibility in the form of knowledge about a certain aspect of work that is not visible to others. This helps not only to recognize the experience and knowledge of each of the team members but also to use their "different field of vision" for various aspects of required team tasks, including decision-making.

A good example is UNU, an online platform that people can use to interact and solve problems as an artificial swarm intelligent unit. Members have used the platform to predict the outcomes of many social events, including sports, the person of the year, and directions of industry movements. The process implemented in UNU includes integrating noisy inputs, weighing alternatives in real time, and converging on decisions; individuals can use UNU as "agents" of swarms and work together to converge on solutions for various problems.

Another great example is the fieldwork performed by Seeley, published in his book in 2010. That research shows how neurological brains and swarms, such as swarms of honeybees, have similar decision-making processes. I will elaborate on this research much more later.

Intelligent Teams can certainly benefit from applying similar principles in AFSA and processes implemented in UNU to improve decision-making and integrate scopes of vision as model parameters. With some training, team members will be applying simple functions so they can focus on what needs to be done, including work, research, learning, knowledge-building, and training. The team setup should provide adequate fields of vision for all team members to become direct contributors to all teamwork aspects.

Learning From Fireflies

Our house used to be backed by a ravine that housed a swarm of fireflies. In the summer, you could just sit in the backyard and look at the mesmerizing lights from these little "fairies." Fireflies use their lights for practical purposes, such as basic survival and communicating with each other. They turn their lights on and off in fast sequences that mean something different according to what they feel. Sometimes, it's the most basic form of attracting a mate, but sometimes, they signal to warn against approaching predators, as well as when they find a source of food. The short and rhythmic flashes have various meanings depending on their intensity and frequency. To understand the behavior of a firefly swarm, which can be quite complicated, and to apply the principles, though, researchers consider a simplified artificial firefly.

This simplified agent is unisex. The flashings of light are used for various functions. The underlying function is defined by the objective, but the model uses the higher brightness of the flash to show attractiveness. Based on this model, researchers can design a simple algorithm to compare the position of each firefly as they move around; if a firefly is positioned better (as known by the brightness of flashes the firefly produces), other fireflies will move toward the brighter one.

This model is used in network optimizations, traffic directions, and logistics, just to name a few. For our purposes, this model can be quite beneficial in setting rules and processes for Intelligent Teams. Here is how: Team members can use this behavior by offering their stances or points of view on a situation. This is a bit different from other models because team members will observe and study other members' points of view and check the relative rational information to vote for another member's idea or optimize their own point of view. Once done, they will review the information and stances of others, eventually selecting the best stance.

New research shows that fireflies can form groups within their swarms. It means that they can distinguish between sub-swarms within the same area. This capability plays right into our mindset of having multiple teams to work alongside each other and achieve their common goals together and collaborate on their groups' specific goals. The way to introduce this concept in our team-building approach is to have these groups or sub-colonies set up teams in parallel and assign agents to communicate information across the teams. However, we can also regard these "sub-teams" as an indication of a few people establishing groups to enforce their own ideas. If this sounds familiar, it is because it is a form of groupthink, which we have talked about extensively so far, and we should try to avoid. So, if the subgroups are by design and we want to have parallel threads of solutions and progress to come up with new methods and approaches, it's good, but team members forming subgroups to push their desired approach is groupthink and needs to be avoided.

The simple form of fireflies' behavior has been used in the form of algorithms for various purposes. These examples include business process optimizations, maximum outputs of a potential project, or choosing between available options given the limited resources (i.e., deciding between choices). The observed behaviors in firefly swarms show us that we may be able to go after multiple options possible, without prejudice, and allow sub-teams to come up with their own version of the solution and then "co-evaluate" the best possible option.

We can, of course, change this simpler form of firefly behavior and combine it with other stochastic models to generate other alternatives, and then use computer simulations to evaluate the performance of potentially better routines. In other words, and applying this principle to our team management, we can encourage this behavior in members of the team to take part in evaluating the options provided by other members and understand their perspectives. In this way, the best segments of each solution can be extracted, and an even better option may emerge. Hence, this approach can be applied to

- idea generation in teams, provided by individuals or sub-teams,
- decision-making processes, and
- optimization of business solutions.

Learning From Wolves

You can visit conservation areas in Canada dedicated to wolves. There is one in Haliburton, Ontario. You can observe packs of wolves from behind a thick glass. The design of the center is such that the wolves are not disturbed or aware of their curious visitors. Wolves live in packs, and each pack does have an alpha male. The true story of how the alpha becomes the leader is less about domination by fighting and more about mating and having pups that constitute the pack. I am not going to talk about that much here or go through the psychoanalysis of an alpha personality. However, certain behaviors in a pack of wolves are interestingly applicable to building a successful Intelligent Team.

There are three main species of wolves: Grey, Red, and Timber. There are also 40 different subspecies. Each of these presents various group behaviors. The one interesting for our purpose is the search for prey. Nearly all the wolf species demonstrate this behavior: the pack divides. Each wolf starts searching for the prey. When hunger strikes, the pack becomes a synchronized hunting machine. Once the prey is found, the more experienced ones, usually the alpha pair, lead the charge. During the charge, they use howling and various types of barks to communicate with each other, and they also use visual cues. One interesting behavior is harmonizing their howling, which helps to create an illusion of a larger pack. They also use movements and body language to send each other messages.

The one behavior in all of the hunting process that is most interesting and applicable to teams is the initial search for the prey, which is performed individually but also in alignment within the pack. Each wolf covers a terrain, part of its domain, and in doing so, they send each other messages to let the members of the pack know what they are up to.

Intelligent Team members can benefit from this behavior. If the topic of research is too wide, it can be broken into pieces, and each member or sub-team (depending on the team size) can search for answers and solutions. We are talking about a rather known process: breaking down bigger problems into smaller subproblems, with each member working on a particular subproblem. This principle is applied in project management extensively, but in that discipline, we know what tasks need to be done. Here, we are exploring. We are solving a puzzle, and we do not know what it will look like. The answer or options that each team member or sub-team is going to bring forward will help us put together a solution. From that point of view, it is the reverse of the project management approach. We just know the areas of the unknown and ask the team members to explore each area and uncover facts, challenges, and potential solutions that can then be used to form the final solution. In doing so, when team members find something interesting or a challenge, they will send the signal (howl) so that others can help or adjust their approaches.

The approach used by the packs of wolves can be used as a process by teams who seek a solution that needs collaboration in various areas of expertise. This collaboration can be based on their hierarchy in the pack and includes a hierarchy that starts with a lead wolf and elite scout wolves. When wolves find their prey, they communicate by calling the pack. The wolf pack process uses this calling behavior. Wolves in the wolf pack process summon others when they find prey so that they can close in on it faster and more effectively or adjust their approach for that purpose.

Team members can use the wolf pack process to scout a wide range of possibilities. Once team members discover traces of a better solution, they can use the calling behavior to summon others to evaluate the potential solution. Depending on the team's goals, members could be assigned to seek a solution or receive a subproblem to solve. Once team members find a solution, they can call others to speed up problem resolution or consultation.

These approaches are applicable in hierarchical and flat structures. A variation of the wolf search approach used by gray wolves presents more roles within the hierarchy. Research shows that hierarchy levels in swarm searchers indicate better results than existing organizational hierarchies. Team members can use these findings to facilitate the transition from a traditional hierarchy to a self-managed team while keeping a sense of central control suitable for larger organizations. Wolf search optimizations can provide team members with new methods for choosing the right issues to work on, and members can divide the problem into subproblems so members with more expertise in each area can lead exploration efforts and collaborate on the optimum.

Learning From Ants

There are more than 12,000 ant species. They have been around for more than 150 million years, since the Jurassic period. They live in large colonies. Since childhood, I have been fascinated by how powerful they seem despite their size. Ants can build colossal structures, and the larger colonies can have millions of workers.

One of the early books I read about ants was by Belgian playwright Maurice Maeterlinck, called *The Life of an Ant*, first published in 1930. In that book, Maeterlinck explores ant societies, nest-building and foraging behaviors, reproduction, the role of the queen ant, and the interdependence of ants and nature. A particular area that Maeterlinck explored was the ants' intelligence and communication. He questioned whether ants had a different level of intelligence.

We now know that most of the communications happen through chemical signals (pheromones). Faster and more direct communication happen through touching the antennae. Ants can pass lots of information using the number of taps, which can indicate the size of the food or predator. They can also use sounds to communicate. The process, called stridulation, produces a sound by rubbing parts of the ant's abdomen together. This sound is mostly used for sending danger or warning signals. This "howling" of the ants can travel up to 100 feet! More accurate technologies have shown that ants can also sense the slightest vibrations, so they do seem to communicate through that as well.

That intelligence that Maeterlinck was pointing out is what we call swarm intelligence. Ants have had millions of years to perfect their methods, and we should see how they use those methods to communicate so well. There is a lot to learn here.

One of the well-researched skills of an ant colony is their ability to solve problems. They seem to be able to find the shortest route between two points and adjust their way when things change. It seems mysterious, but once you know how it works, it's quite fascinating yet simple. Ants use pheromones to communicate with each other, as each leaves a trail of pheromones as it forages for food. Eventually, the shorter or more successful path to food receives more pheromones and becomes the preferred choice.

Research in the 1990s demonstrated how individuals can use this behavior to solve optimization problems, such as the traveling salesman problem (choosing the shortest route to travel between destinations). The method involves a communication mechanism, the usage of experience, and making decisions accordingly. This approach is interesting to us because we want to enable team members to act like an ant colony and share knowledge, experience, exploratory results, and lessons learned from the past. Ants communicate their preferences after walking a passage; team members can use the same concept to propose an option or weigh in on a concept or option offered by others.

More recent research used the ant colony approach for optimization to solve scheduling problems, vehicle routing problems, and assignment problems (pairing items based on particular conditions and desired outcomes). The ant colony optimization approach uses two elements to determine the probability of a certain choice: accumulation of pheromones on each option and visibility of success. So, in each possible option, either we look at how our past experiences (frequency of success or indication of a higher/better possibility) match with the situation and/or we rely on new evidence of achieving success. The latter is specifically useful if we are solving a new problem or if something has changed. For example, even though we have evidence that doing something in a certain way has always paid off, if there is a change, a new technique, or the removal of an obstacle, may give us a clearly better passage to success. The result of the comparison between the ant colony optimization-based approach in solving selection decision-making processes and traditional approaches had over a 95% success rate (Ghasab et al., 2015).

How should we apply the ant colony's approach to Intelligent Team's work? When team members reach a decision-making point or need to generate options, they can use lessons learned and experience to make a selection in the same way ant colony optimization shows passage preference due to pheromone accumulation. This part takes care of the pheromone component. Ants' visibility of their surroundings can be mapped to organizational knowledge, personal knowledge, and knowledge gained during the performance of the current or recent tasks. To do this effectively, our Intelligent Team needs to have access to the history of past projects and contribute to it as more projects are completed. Team members also need to be able to have discussions to share their personal knowledge and experience, perhaps from the past while in other organizations, to be added to the organizational knowledge.

Recent studies showed that ants use different types of pheromones that are produced by various glands, and each pheromone lasts for a specific time. Ants use their pheromones to expand their communication to include information about currently active trails and depleting food sources. Forager ants use short-lasting pheromones when they want to attract sufficient nest-mates to collect prey and use the long-lasting pheromone to lead other ants to longer-lasting food sources, such as a patch of desirable plants. For example, short-lived pharaoh ant pheromones last 20 minutes, and long-lasting pheromones can last for days. Ants use other pheromones as alarm mechanisms to indicate the urgency of decision-making. Ants use this mechanism to choose the best path based on this signal or similar ones or to continue based on their knowledge (e.g., to explore other passages). We can replicate this method by allowing team members to vote on particular options, as well as assigning a higher and lower priority on decisions.

The application of the behavior of ant colonies to optimize their foraging and dealing with threats has expanded to image processing and edge detection (an algorithm used by photo processing software to identify various objects in a picture). For the ants, it's about setting the boundaries of foraging, but for information technology, it has become a method of how humans search for information (information foraging theory). In a way, humans also use information scents (cues) to follow a threat, to continue to read or to decide whether to click on a link or not. In information foraging theory, individuals display the same behaviors as animal foragers when they look for information online. In 2016, the researchers Drias and Pasi used ant colony optimization to indicate the similarity between web surfers and ant foraging. They applied ant colony optimization to a real website with search words and quickly found relevant results.

Using this concept, team members can use ant colony optimization to gain an understanding of the full picture, such as why they are working on various projects or even sub-projects of a larger one, and how they fit in overall goals and objectives, thus establishing a general sense of cohesiveness to achieve all team targets while avoiding pitfalls and wandering among false targets.

Decision-Making in Honeybees

Honeybees display some of the most amazing behaviors that we may be able to apply to our Intelligent Team's setup. They face many challenges, from finding nests to foraging and dealing with threats to their nests. Because humans have had a close relationship with honeybees, perhaps we know more about them and their behaviors than about any other social beings in nature.

As such, I will focus on two decision-making behaviors and examine fieldwork and models of how bees perform their tasks. Bees use the first behavior, foraging behavior, to select areas around their nests for maximum efficiency. The second behavior is the process of selecting a new nest. Perhaps a major note here is to mention that the queen bee does not play a role in these important functions. The role of the queen is to keep the bees together by pheromones and then to produce eggs to expand the colony and, at times, to produce more queens.

Foraging behavior is a critical bee swarm function. Scholars have widely studied bee swarm functions and have utilized the resulting models in various applications. These behaviors are used to build simpler algorithms. Artificial bee colony algorithms present data on three types of bees in the colony: scouts, foragers, and onlookers. Scouts go out of the hive to locate sources of food. Experienced scouts combine historical information about the location and quality of food sources (cognitive knowledge) with scouts' input (social knowledge). Foragers are female (they are called female but cannot reproduce) and have the responsibility of collecting food. Onlookers have the important duty of protecting the nest against various dangers, like predators. When they are not busy, onlookers protect scouts on their missions. Onlooker bees use elevated social knowledge (after experienced foragers combine social knowledge with cognitive knowledge) to consider their next trip. Artificial bee colony algorithms have vast applications in software engineering, telecommunications, mechanical and civil engineering, data mining, image processing, and industrial engineering.

Experienced bees evaluate their cognitive and social knowledge in each decision-making round. Onlooker bees and scouts use the innate built-in "algorithm" to choose a destination for food collection or look for prospect locations. In reality, it's not easy to fully follow all the bees and find out how they behave, although, in recent years, technology has come to help in the form of video analysis software tools or simulations. For example, using the principles of the observed behaviors and simulating them in optimization software, the researchers sought to solve job scheduling problems. Some of the findings are especially interesting for our portfolio of behaviors in Intelligent Teams. In the approach, the researchers added multiple objectives to the algorithm, meaning each scout could be looking for more than one goal or objective, being the source of food, water, and maybe the location of the next nest. Then, they assumed that scouts were divided into two groups. Scouts in one group advocate for the locations discovered up to that point, and scouts in the other group continue searching for potentially better locations. This is more or less what happens in real honeybee scouts. Some of them are constantly searching for new resources, and some go for verification, although we don't necessarily know the proportion of scouts dedicated to each task.

One of the ways we can apply this to improve teamwork is the team members' approach to solving problems. Part of the team can start working on a solution while the rest can continue exploring better options. In that way, we can make progress while still being on the lookout for potentially better options. There is an implied risk and cost here. If the solution that is being worked on is not the optimal solution, once the better one is discovered, we may need to redo all of the work, and at the same time, if it is the best solution, then we are losing part of the workforce searching for something that we won't find. This set of risks and costs will be there anyway, but as you will see, we will be able to minimize them.

The next interesting thing that honeybees do fascinatingly is the decision process when they are ready to choose a new nest. At times, most of the bees and the current queen leave the nest and leave the old one to the new queen. The oldest and most experienced scouts (accounting for 300 to 500 of every 10,000 bees in an average colony) that had the role of foraging up to that point are dispatched from the hive to look for new nest locations (Figure 6.1). We did not know much about this process until the research done by Seeley in 2010.

That research confirmed that scouts mainly investigate the overall size, entrance size, and direction of the potential nest's opening (north is preferable) in their search. They fly out in all directions and can go different distances before they find what they may consider a proper potential for the new nest. They then fly back to the colony and present their discovery to the rest. Here is when it gets very interesting. They have to communicate the size, direction, and distance and basically make their case to the rest of the community! The way they do it is by performing a waggle dance. For example, one second of dance is equivalent to one kilometer. New video technologies have helped researchers make these measurements and show how the overall process works. Scouts may repeat their advertising movements every 30 minutes, each advocating and promoting what they found based on their observations.

This is a long process and usually takes days. As time passes by, more scouts go and "check out" the locations and come back and join the promotion of one of their choices; that is, they start the same dance or "vote" for that option. Toward the end of the process, everyone has checked out the preferred location, and they are all doing the same dance. A consensus has been reached. That day will be the moving day!

Humans rarely reach a consensus. In fact, it is usually reserved for very small teams or specific settings like jury members, where all of them should agree with simplified versions of the outcome, usually "guilty" and "not guilty." We can decide to have everyone on board with a particular business decision, but differences will most of the time remain, and consensus is extremely hard to achieve.

Although scouts do not visit all the potential nest options presented, they do visit certain sites and may choose to continue advertising their original site or move to support another. Seeley concluded that scouts communicate the quality of the new nest through the strength of their dances (higher duration and frequency). Scouts follow a "retire and rest" pattern after presenting their findings and visiting other potential nest sites. Unlike some people, bees stop pushing for their options when other bees discover new, better ideas.

Seeley also demonstrated that bees make decisions not on consensus but on quorum. He placed multiple nests close to each other. Although bees in the swarm took longer to decide on a nest, in the end, they chose one, and all bees moved in. Bees have to consider a balance between the speed of decision and accuracy. This is a survival matter for the bees in the swarm, as

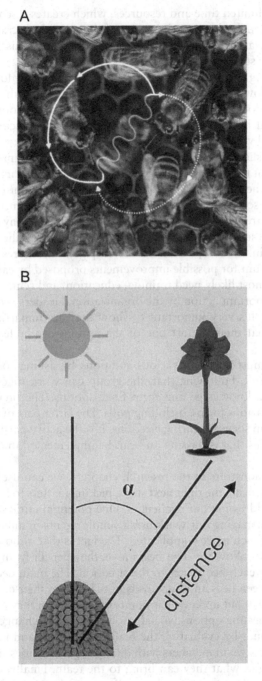

Figure 6.1 Honeybee waggle dance

they may face limited time and resources, which creates a sense of urgency. On its own, though, this is perhaps one of the most democratic displays of nature, and toward the end of this chapter, I will include this as a major lesson learned for structuring the Intelligent Team.

The next thing the bee colony has to do is move to a new location. It's the moving day. However, by that day, only a small fraction (about 4%) of the bees know the location of the new nest. This process is another fascinating event displayed by the honeybee scouts and was only discovered in 2006 using advanced video processing techniques.

Scouts start showing the way to the rest of the bee swarm by flying very fast at the top of the colony, then slowly flying back to the back of the swarm and repeating the routine. This resembles an arrow to point out the way to the others. The scouts fly very fast on top, as fast as 34 kilometers per hour.

In trying to apply the honeybees' approach, members may create a sense of interest. The sense of interest in others' opinions is not alien to us in general; however, in this case, we need to develop genuine interest in everyone's views and account for possible improvements proposed by each team member. That will most likely need training, education, and reminders.

The next important action by the organizational leaders is to reduce their own influence! It's very important to show they are impartial and, if not, demonstrate that theirs is just one of the options available and open for discussion.

Next, they must cultivate various solutions by asking for independent exploratory work. Following that, the group can work together to aggregate the gained knowledge and form final options. The final vote can be conducted in various forms, including polls. The latter part of this process is well exercised in societies during elections. It is the active participation of all interested parties that is missing and can be implemented in organizational settings.

As I will demonstrate in the research chapters, we can use the honeybee approach in choosing the right next steps, picking matters to focus on, giving priority, and addressing our challenges. One potential criticism of what we can learn for managing our work using simple agents in intelligent swarms is that we are much more complicated. The fact is that although bees work as a swarm and follow the next best move, they benefit from the skills and experience that each bee brings to the situation. The main decision-making difference between bees and humans is how bees use their experience (cognitive knowledge) but update their points of view when they learn about the latest food or nesting options (social knowledge). Bees change their options without resistance by evaluating the reality of options and newly acquired knowledge. Thus, team members with different personalities should learn to accept others and what they can bring to the team. Finally, bees' constant lookout for better options shows how self-managed teams and organization-wide employees should continuously search for improvement to move toward becoming a learning organization.

Learning From Cuckoo's Search

Cuckoos lay their eggs in the nests of other species. Some species of cuckoos have even adopted the shape, color, and pattern of their preferred hosts' eggs. Cuckoos search nearby areas but fly far to search other neighborhoods, increasing the possibility of finding a suitable nest. To imagine this better, think about random lines representing a local search and long lines between them as the bird moves to a new area for search.

Cuckoos may find a few new potentials and some older sites. To optimize their findings, they may fly longer distances at random to cover wider areas and quickly find new opportunities.

This behavior has already attracted computer scientists' attention. Some have applied it in search algorithms. Some have used it in image processing, neural network training for AI tools, spam detection, and feature selection.

The egg in the cuckoo search is the equivalent of a solution to a problem. If the hosting bird discovers the cuckoo's egg, it will discard the egg (i.e., the solution is not the best option). However, the cuckoo invests in laying many eggs, sometimes up to 50. That aspect of the real world could be hard to apply because, in reality, the team will most likely not be able to try more than a few solutions.

There is no known standard approach for team members to search for solutions due to the nature of problem-solving. However, members should be equipped with such approaches so other members can achieve their objectives. In other words, team members should use cuckoo search to pursue options and solutions instead of searching for options and solutions randomly. That way, they can use how cuckoos choose a nest (a solution) with the highest prospect of success. Team members need first to identify the parameters of the problem. Then, each team member should attempt to solve the problem, which may involve choosing the priority of work features (or any other problems). Team members then explore the advantages or disadvantages of the potential solution. After that, they examine the potential solution in a range of parameters and can dramatically change the parameters (levy flight) to find potential solutions in that vicinity. The team may compare their initial solutions with new potential solutions, refine the active solution set, and continue until they present their findings. Then, they can compare and contrast their findings with each other and come up with the best solution.

Hence, the key advantage of using cuckoo's approach manifests in the different initial approaches taken by different team members, which can help in cataloging more potential options.

Decision-Making in Intelligent Teams Using Biomimicking

Since humans evolved in groups, they are familiar with living with others and making decisions together. We may think that we have come a long way and can do much better than before. The fact is that everything we have to decide about has also become far more complicated, and the amount of data, correct or incorrect, relevant or not, has also increased by many factors. We can choose to continue with traditional methods of group discussions; however, inefficiencies in group decision-making cause a loss of opportunities. There are proven deficiencies in humans' cognitive minds that lead to suboptimal decisions. Back in 2017, psychology researchers Tindale and Kameda pointed out the increasing importance of evolutionary theory in understanding human social behavior. Postulating similarities between humans and social animals, they recommended comparative research across species to get a united and informed understanding of group decision-making processes. They evaluated how humans use collective wisdom and social sharing to modify group behavior. These tools help avoid missed opportunities in the forms of motivational behavior or coordination losses common in human groups but not in social beings like bees. That's what I am referring to here in this book: an outline of the learned behavior of social beings to support a better understanding of teams' setup and functions, with a focus on the decision-making process.

One principle is that the people close to an underlying subject where a decision is required can make better decisions about the subject. Accuracy diminishes when larger groups of people who may not be as close to the problem get involved. In general, we know that large crowds can usually provide a better prediction than a small group. However, research has shown that people in swarm-like situations where closed feedback loops exist act better and make more accurate predictions than people in larger crowds. Also, various studies have shown that team members can find better solutions than when members higher in the hierarchy do not dictate decisions from outside the team.

As noted in the review of simplified processes used by social beings, team members can apply basic rules and mechanisms to address even the most complicated problems. For example, bats use echolocation to identify the locations of their prey and other bats while avoiding various obstacles. Bats make decisions and perform corrective actions while using echolocation. This process presents highly optimized decision-making routines that Intelligent Team members can use for various selections and decisions.

Bats' behavior is used in the form of an algorithm in various applications. It is a complicated routine but can be simplified by reducing the parameters to consider, also known as attribute reduction. The application of these routines helps with improving decision-making processes in two ways: first, by helping team members choose between available options based on known problem attributes, and second, by helping them recognize selection parameter patterns and providing a higher-level view that otherwise might be hard to distinguish. In other words, team members will be able to focus on what matters and then seek how the relationships between those parameters work to come up with the best possible solution.

As pointed out before, this is the first effort to apply swarm intelligence and biomimicking in management and leadership, but scholars have used similar techniques in different areas of science and for different applications. For example, a combination of swarm intelligence and financial routines has been used to provide an online system for employees in financial groups who make financial predictions. The increased performance of these predictions using swarm intelligence indicated two main points aligned with this book. First, members of intelligent swarms help each other make better predictions under uncertainty, and second, team members can use simple models, such as online collaboration systems, to interact and share key data and increase everyone's success rate. Sharing personal points of view for prediction aggregation is a step toward group decision-making and can be a basis for an approach to effective team decisions.

There is an opposing concern in equalizing humans and simpler social beings in that humans think and behave differently from nonhuman agents in a swarm. Two major counterpoints in this argument are worth mentioning: First, I am not proposing the removal of emotions and complicated behaviors in humans. I am proposing a unification of behavior when it comes to certain actions like decision-making. This is not about ignoring the complications; it is about separating them and equalizing with other team members on the approach when needed. Second, there are behavioral differences in social beings as well, meaning they can do what they do despite individual uniqueness and variability. For example, one particular research studying the behaviors of groups of birds, such as green woodhoopoes, and mammals, such as meerkats and dwarf mongooses, shows that there is attention to all members of the swarm but focuses on essential routines related to survival. We can define and use a notion of parameter, for example, the confidence level in dealing with a hard situation, as proposed by the research, and expect better outcomes (Marshall et al., 2017). This is a great entry point to include higher levels of human cognitive minds in this book. Given the differences between team members' personalities, backgrounds, and overall frames of reference, human team members need more complicated considerations when they choose between available options and decision-making processes. The inclusion of behavioral differences will provide leaders with opportunities to use swarm intelligence to come up with better decision-making models.

Intelligent Team Implementation Strategies Using Biomimicking and Swarm Intelligence

It's time to put together a set of implementation strategies based on swarm intelligence.

Learning from bats that move toward their prey among many other bats by constantly surveying the environment and the positions of others and their prey and deciding the next move based on that, for example, is a point in setting such strategies. Bat's approach to solving a complicated problem can show us a way to change awareness and communication behavior, show the importance of decision-making in teams, and emphasize the need for consultation with team members.

We can learn from the fish swarm that we need to have an overview vision, as well as the importance of goal orientation. The behavior of fireflies in alerting others about a desirable or unwanted situation shows us the necessity of subgrouping and the importance of generating more alternatives for decision-making. Learning from wolves can help leaders of organizations implement Intelligent Teams within their hierarchies. Using the simple rules from ant colonies, teams can learn how to stay on course and be cohesive within the teams. Finally, decision-making in honeybees when moving to a new nest can be mapped to a guide for making complicated decisions, providing decision behaviors to investigate options, the importance of getting feedback from all team members, dividing teams into smaller groups, and validating the decisions by constantly evaluating the changes and surroundings.

For leaders to set up their teams based on the learned disciplines of non-human social beings and intelligent swarms, members should exhibit the following behaviors:

- Understand the overall team function, goals, and required tasks.
- Respond to internal and external changes collectively.
- Understand and plan for emergencies.
- Understand the equality of all members and feel comfortable opining on team activities.
- Know about end goals and periodically check for internal or external system changes. Team members strive to stay in alignment with other team members. In this way, team members can make small corrections to stay on track.
- Understand that, due to different frames of reference, certain team members may need more time to reach the same level of understanding. They should collaborate to reach the same degree of understanding or move in the same direction in thought processes. Team members with closer points of view and those with different ideas should consult with each other frequently.
- Iteratively share information and communicate changes.
- Because team members may have different perspectives, they should constantly transfer knowledge to ensure information distribution.
- Consider team members' experience, organizational knowledge, and lessons learned from past tasks, and prioritize and validate options presented through experience.

In addition, team members must follow a series of steps in making a decision. These are:

- Break down the problem into smaller subproblems with few and preferably binary options and discuss the best choice with all team members. Team members will continue to solve other problems until they find a clear solution to the main problem.

- Communicate alternatives and discuss choices iteratively to reach a stronger acceptance of the decision.
- Discover and present potential solutions, and invite team members to explore them. Team members should advocate for the strongest solutions, regardless of who first presented them, checking other solutions with open minds.
- Divide into subgroups to find different potential solutions if team members cannot find clear alternatives. Team members exchange subgroups to trigger innovation.
- Opine on selected solutions and change parameters to discover a potentially stronger solution variation.
- Once team members select a solution, they continue to explain the approach to others who do not understand or are not able to take part in the discussion for any reason.

ENTERING THE UNCHARTED TERRITORIES

Scholars and industry leaders have studied teams and team behaviors from various perspectives; however, before this book and the research it is based on, we did not have an inclusive method for team decision-making. There have been some efforts, such as proposed guidelines by Liff and Gustavson in 2016, focusing on the implementation of self-managed or self-governed teams; however, these high-level guidelines do not provide solutions to the challenges that leaders setting up effective teams need to address.

There has been limited research on why teams tend to be successful or struggle with challenges, but research has focused on very few aspects, such as goal orientation, empowerment, humility, stewardship, accountability, communication, team dynamics, conflicts, and interpersonal relationships. There is an opportunity here to learn from intelligent swarms to set aside all those differences and focus on behaviors that can help the team make the best possible choices on and on.

We also need to have a solid decision-making process different from the traditional one that suits the proposed Intelligent Team. It is going to be based on a self-managed team approach but using intelligent swarms to rectify the challenges that have pinned down such teams so far. The expected implementation process shows resolve and addresses the lack of a traditional decision-maker in self-governing teams. Aspects that have effects on decision-making processes in such teams include information availability, team member participation, addressing the roles of leaders and facilitators, division of design, and technical aspects. Such a solution should be able to address existing significant challenges such as groupthink, lack of synergy, and organizational goal alignment.

Intelligent Team implementation requires devising new approaches to problem-solving, revising existing activities, and inventing new ways of doing activities. I compiled a set of behaviors to simulate how nonhuman social beings execute leaderless collaboration in nature. With these in mind, I set out research to see what we can learn from teams that already exhibit most of what we deem to be successful behaviors and what works best. A constant consideration in the research, which I will explain in the next chapter, was to learn the optimized behavior and bring it into a process for an effective team I've been calling the Intelligent Team.

Part 3

The Research

Chapter 7

Research
Data Gathering and Analysis

I wanted to see how teams were set up in companies, especially if they were given the self-managed or self-governing designation because that seems to be how successful intelligent swarms operate. My specific interest was to see how they made decisions because, without a designated manager or with a manager who follows the principles of a self-managed team, which is a necessity if everyone is participating as equally as possible, how would the teams make decisions and how they correct the path if necessary? In doing so, I needed to find a place that had multiple self-managed teams to be able to have as much in common across the teams as possible, such as overall leadership team, company culture, pay rates, and so on. I also wanted a fast-paced environment where external factors changed, so the company approach and strategy had to have coping mechanisms with strategic or tactical responses to the market. These requirements presented themselves in a technology company that will be known to us as Sigma Corporation. Sigma had multiple teams, so as the first step, I reviewed how these teams functioned and chose three teams that most closely matched the criteria of the research. By that, I mean these teams were applying most of what is known as a successful self-governing team. I was going to find out how much they resembled an intelligent swarm's behavior and, obviously, how much I could learn from them to solidify a set of approaches, routines, and strategies for building and operating Intelligent Teams.

RESEARCH SETUP

I set up a qualitative multi-case study. Greek philosophers such as Protagoras, Plato, and Aristotle used qualitative inquiry to find strategies and methods to seek a common perception among different perspectives. Qualitative inquiry provides opportunities to learn the meanings of human experiences, study how things work, capture people's perceptions and experiences, understand the context, identify unanticipated consequences, and, specific to the case study design, discover patterns and themes across cases. The diversity of cases allows various aspects to be brought forward and helps to extract

DOI: 10.1201/9781003527206-10

hidden information and compare. In my study, I used three cases for the teams, each team ranging between 4 and 10 team members, which I'll refer to as teams A, B, and C.

The actual data collection was done through conducting semi-structured interviews. I had shared the interview questions with the team members ahead of time, so they had time to review them beforehand. The questions were about how people thought about their teamwork experience. The advantage that multiple cases brought to the research was replication and reinforcement of evidence and ideas. The context of each team, team members' underlying work, and teams' dynamics were slightly different, providing a framework of triangulation and discovery of slight factors that meant a lot in the end.

Another source of information in this research was organizational records. I needed to know how successful each team was in terms of company measurements and metrics, meeting budgets and timelines, performance indicators, and so on. I used these to compare the team members' input with the actual, tangible, measured outcomes of each team. Details of the research are published in the *International Journal of Development Research* (Nozari and Shuttler, 2021).

Another noteworthy fact is that the teams were working in technology, the pace of change was high, and work cycles were comparatively short. Due to the high competition, ease of entry into the market, and constant technology change, the design of teams and work should align with those environmental factors. Organizational leaders have to constantly search for improvement in the throughput of their teams, and employee retention matters even more.

QUESTIONS AND WHY THEY MATTERED

I wanted to know about the experience of team members working in their respective teams. I also wanted to know about how they functioned within the team, as true self-managed teams are hard to come by, and there are lots of challenges about basic activities, but mostly, how they made decisions. I was looking to see how they presented their experience; that is, as a team that functioned beyond individuals and presented attributes of an intelligent swarm, or as individuals who were looking at others for making decisions, or somewhere in between.

Data Analysis

After completing the interviews, I started data analysis using manual coding. Soon, a few interesting patterns started to appear. At the highest level, I had input on how much experience the team members had in working in self-managed teams, how much they understood about team settings, their team processes, and how they did their job, communications, and, of course, the decision-making process.

The level of experience within the current job and working within self-managed team settings is important. Obviously, another factor to consider was the general experience of team players at their current or similar jobs. It was clear that working in their team settings, it mattered how much of the overall strategy and goals they knew because it could affect their decisions. They also admitted that individuals with expertise in certain areas could make better suggestions, which would eventually transform into a decision, making them the subject matter experts on the topic. They also emphasized that they all participated in the decision-making process, which allowed a diversity of ideas as the input of that process.

Autonomy was another emergent topic in data analysis. The participants liked the fact that they could make decisions about the priority of what they worked on. Team members enjoyed how they were able to choose the solutions to the problems they were trying to solve. More than a few mentioned that they liked this aspect of their job so much that they wouldn't accept higher-paid jobs elsewhere.

In terms of overall feeling, many of the team members seem happy to share about the successes of their teams. Participants were using phrases like "happier here," "excited about the work I am doing," and "enjoying my job like never before." Many were talking about a sense of belonging and being seen and valued for the first time in their careers. They were simply expressing what the industry calls job satisfaction.

Team members across cases A, B, and C noted they were getting things done faster, with more efficiency, higher quality, and better outcomes. It seemed participants were quick to bring up that they were highly motivated and wanted to stay with their team, which is not usually the case in the technology sector where high salary offers are not unusual.

Many of the participants brought up that since they started the new team settings, trust among team members had gone up. They felt they could be open with their teammates and trusted that, at least from the workplace environment, it was a cordial and safe place, which led to more engagement by everyone on the team.

Another interesting revelation was that the constraint of work was not forgotten. Nearly everyone brought up that they still have to be on time, on budget, deliver the requested scope of work, and do it all with limitations of their team's size and available human resources.

It wasn't all vanilla sky in the feedback from the team members. However, interestingly, while mentioning the drawbacks, participants indicated how their teams were organized to overcome each challenging situation. In other words, expected challenges were appearing, but with the team setup, they mostly knew what to do about them. The feedback was not that the team setup was wrong or that the concept of self-management wasn't working. Instead, they were about difficulties that are part of the

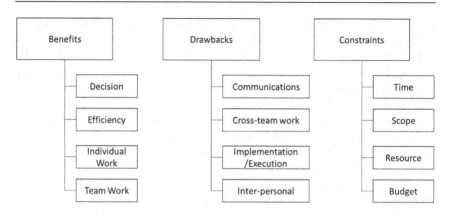

Figure 7.1 Benefits, drawbacks, and constraints factors

job but might have been augmented as a result of their particular team setting, which had higher risks of exposure. For example, they'd point out how they were expecting the communications to happen and what they'd do to avoid communication failure or teach each other how to avoid the pitfalls of communication.

They also pointed out that working with other teams when cross-collaboration was needed presented challenges. There were some issues with implementation, as well as interpersonal challenges.

Evaluation of success is a combination of the participant's evaluation, the constraints, and the reality of measurements performed and monitored by the company. Figure 7.1 shows the categories of benefits, drawbacks, and constraints of the participating company's self-managed team.

To understand the work structure and how work was done, I looked at responses from two different angles:

1. Tasks: These are the activities that sum up what the team is expected to accomplish.
2. Collaboration: These point out the dynamics of collaboration between the team members. Many of them pointed to a facilitator who was sometimes filled by one of the team members or, from time to time, by an outsider.

Figure 7.2 shows these categories and themes.

Core Processes

For any team to function, it needs to have a set of rules that govern how team members will actually get things done (core process). If we use the analogy of an engine, for example, its main function is to convert various

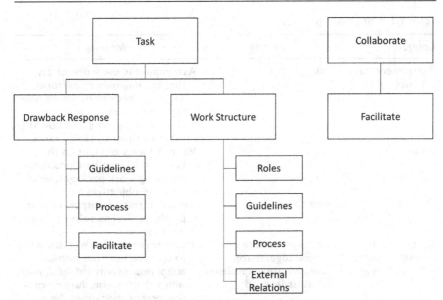

Figure 7.2 **Structure for task and collaboration factors**

sources of energy into mechanical energy. For the team, it's going to be how team members produce their required output, which could be anything like a design, software, improvement of the health of a patient, manufacturing high-quality products, or customer satisfaction.

Two subprocesses are highly important for improving team performance: communication and decision-making. The communication process determines how team members transmit and receive information between themselves, as well as to and from outside the team. The topic of communications is a key success determination factor in all the fields and aspects of business, so much so that it appears as a challenging or strength factor of every conversation about possible improvements, project postmortems, and company reorganizations.

Decision-making is the next key subprocess, with augmented importance in this book, as we intend to build a team, an Intelligent Team, that can make most, if not all, of its decisions within. Traditionally, decisions are made by someone like a manager based on their experience and judgment. Some managers consult within the team, and some just rely on the facts and figures available to them. If the problem at hand is complicated and the decision will have major financial implications, they may build a decision board, listing the pros and cons of each option, and choose the solution that provides the highest favorable outcome. They may also assign weights to each category or factor, so the decision is based on a score toward whichever option produces higher gains (more on this in the next chapter).

Table 7.1 Core team process

Category	Setting	Meaning
Assignment, task revise	Task	Assignment is the work or task that team members perform. Tasks get revised based on how team members are aware of changes happening and how they react to them to revise tasks.
Input	Goal	Various forms of input to the team, which can be a problem, including work packages, metrics, and objectives.
Output	Team Output	Various forms of output, such as products, design, software, and metrics.
Responsibility, team dynamics, process steps	Plan, alignment, team, knowledge, share, collaborate, experience, lessons learned	These are factors outside of elementary functions on how team members accept responsibility and get aligned with each other, plan, share information, increase their knowledge, work as a Team, expand their experience, add to their lessons learned, and collaborate to get the job done.

Back to the core process, I was looking for special activities, settings, arrangements, and structures that were utilized by the team members to perform their job. Table 7.1 shows a summary of what a core process may entail.

You will notice that the core process, at a high level, is a function. Tasks are activities that fulfill the function, with goals and workforce being inputs, and the output of the team is achieving all or parts of the goals. In doing so, we need to make sure the "soft" parts are there to support the basic functions, such as plan, alignment, collaboration, and learning.

Core Process Categories and Subthemes

Next, we will focus on two subfunctions mentioned earlier: communications and decision-making.

Communication Process

Communication is a critical activity in teamwork. Through the communication process, team members share various types of information essential for them to know, learn, collaborate, and work together toward the team's goals. Table 7.2 summarizes how the teams in the study perceived communications.

On the value of communications, participants indicated that proper communication establishes a cadence, allowing them to "know things are

Table 7.2 Communications process categories and subcategories

Category	Subcategory	Meaning
Contents	Contents	Concepts that need to be communicated.
Input, get feedback, work	Internal exchange	Team members seek input or get feedback for their internal teamwork.
Value	Value	The feedback participants provided indicated the value of communication.
Inform, feedback, request, work	External exchange	External communication is used to inform external stakeholders, provide feedback, request something, or work with other teams.
Website, presentation, demo, email, channel	External medium	Team members use websites, presentations, application demos, emails, and communication channels to interact with external teams.
Boards, channels, meetings, direct	Tools	Tools are used to make communications happen.
Frequency	High/medium/low communications	Main team meetings that happen at different intervals. All feedback fits into daily, twice-weekly, or weekly categories.
Role	Breadth	How much of the team members' work involves communicating with other roles and teams?

progressing," to have the "best visibility," as "any misunderstanding gets corrected." Team members would go to other team members to understand what they need to do as input to their work and get feedback. Team members extensively use message boards to establish channels for the whole team, subgroups to discuss a particular topic, and communication with external stakeholders. They can also use tools such as phones, face-to-face conversations, and meetings to communicate.

Decision Process

In making decisions, team members consider various inputs. Some of the items include scalability of products, ease of maintenance, "amount of time we need to work on something," and if "customers are suffering." Inputs to the decision process were categorized into growth, usability, cost, sizing, and complexity. These were rolled up to the decision factors and categories. Team members use various tools in the decision process, including sharing sites, boards, and websites that facilitate voting. These tools are common across the three cases in the study. The decision factors are inputs to the decision process. Table 7.3 shows the categories and themes for the decision process.

Table 7.3 Decision process: categories and themes

Categories	Subcategories	Meaning
Breakdown	Breakdown	Team members break down a problem into smaller pieces to understand it better and find the answers before making decisions.
Strengthen	De-risk, review, retrospective	Team members have methods for reviewing the decisions they have made to strengthen them. They also try to de-risk them by testing their decision results as early as possible. They also review their decisions in retrospective meetings to learn from their approach.
Discover options	Discover, investigate, aid, prototyping	Team members discover options through discussions, investigation, getting help from others, consulting different sources, and, in some cases, doing a quick prototype to complete their options discovery.
Discuss options	Discuss	Discussion is the main activity to review, revise, and consolidate options.
Opine	Participating	Team members are encouraged to participate and opine on options.
Subgroup	Subgroup	The team is broken into subgroups to research a particular issue.

In making decisions, team members have to respond to challenges that make following the process harder. The challenges were categorized based on participants' feedback. Two themes appeared: personal and technical. Personal challenges came from categories such as disagreement (team members disagreeing with others in a discussion), groupthink, attachment (team members getting attached to a solution without the right merits and not supported by data), and participation (members not participating in discussions for making decisions). On the technical theme, challenges happened when the decision was complicated and broad – categorized under major change – when there was missing information or a lack of ideas on how to approach a problem – categorized under missing info or solutions – or when there was a dependency on other teams or people outside of the team to get something done or provided.

Categorization of responses to these challenges led to three subcategories: collect data, work as a team, and lessons learned. The team members started to collect various forms of data by gathering information, consulting with people, or directly getting feedback from their customer community. To handle some of the personal challenges mentioned earlier, team members used team-building techniques such as strengthening the idea of belonging to the team and team support, categorized under team advocacy, continuing

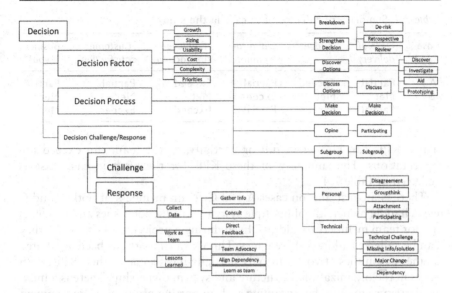

Figure 7.3 Structure for decision factors and categories

to learn from situations categorized under learn-as-team, and working with external stakeholders categorized under align dependency. Figure 7.3 summarizes all categories and subcategories in the decision process.

Performance of Teams in Cases From Participating Company

The participating company leaders had implemented self-managed teams a few years ago. They monitor the progress of the teams via KPIs. Work is done by completing projects. Success is measured through accomplishing KPIs that include the following:

- Projects without a deadline:
  - Claim-to-commit: Has the team been able to claim what they have committed at the time of planning? This indicator is not linear and depends on the number of team members working in the team.
- Projects with a deadline:
  - Date and claim-to-commit
- All projects:
  - Employee satisfaction
  - Budget
  - Business goal: quarterly, claim-to-commit, and date of delivery are linked to business outcomes. The business outcomes depend on sales and customer satisfaction.

Table 7.4 Summary of KPIs for each case in the study

Case	Date of delivery	Budget	Claim-to-commit	Employee satisfaction	Customer satisfaction	Business goal
A	Partial	Exceed	Partial	Exceed	Partial	Partial
B	Met	Met	Exceed	Met	Met	Met
C	Partial	Exceed	Partial	Exceed	Exceed	Met

These KPIs can be met in full or partially, or the team can exceed the expectations. The summary of these KPIs for the team in each case is reflected in Table 7.4.

There is a constraint on cases A and C. Team members of both A and C cases handle ownership of multiple systems. Production issues and incidents are for team members to address. Even during a project with deadlines, they can be called to address these issues. This extra support has been attributed as the reason these two teams only partially meet some of their KPIs, with roots in the organizational structure and system ownership. There is a missing structure to own the sustaining and supporting production environment issues. In the absence of that, these development teams get impacted frequently and miss their KPIs.

Besides that, the team members in Case C have a limited and smaller group of customers. Team members have been able to establish a close relationship with their customer base. Due to a high level of interaction, they get a chance to explain, inform, and collaborate with their customers easier. In this way, they can keep customer satisfaction high. Because of this, they usually negotiate their business goals lower than capacity. Hence, although they meet their dates and claim-to-commit only partially, business goals are met.

In summary, the team in Case B meets or exceeds KPIs and can be deemed successful. Teams in Cases A and C have challenges to deliver on time and deliver on promises. Still, in Case C, the team meets the business goals and gets happier customers by managing their expectations. They deal with the same problems as the team in Case A.

STUDY RESULTS

This section brings two aspects of the study together. These two aspects are biomimicking behaviors in teamwork and decision-making and the description of teamwork and decision-making by team members. By this time in the research, I had categories of data contributing to decision-making, including experience and implementation of self-managed teams, including benefits and drawbacks of the current implementation within each team, and key processes like teamwork and communications. I also had a summary of how these teams perform on their expected KPIs from the company leaders' perspective.

So far, in providing feedback through interview questions, team members who followed biomimicking behaviors seemed to have a good understanding of goals, responded to change collectively, understood the plan, valued the participation of all team members, had internal alignment, collaborated with external resources, shared information frequently, valued experience, and reviewed their work to learn further. Interview questions required participants to describe how they perform their work in self-managed team implementation to see if they aligned with these biomimicking behaviors. In the decision-making process, the biomimicking behavior would be breaking down large items into smaller pieces for easier decision-making, discussing and validating options, striving to discover new options, dividing into subgroups to find new options, opining on solutions presented and participating in discussions, and strengthening decisions by communicating, reviewing, and fixing its issues. In the following sections, using biomimicking behaviors, I present the results of the data analysis.

Experience

Considering experience is a key element in biomimicking behaviors. Experience of team members in each case, working in self-managed teams, working for the company, previous experience of working in self-managed teams, and onboarding the self-managed team in the current company were considered. Previous experience before joining the current company is not much different, but the level of experience working in a self-managed team in Case B is more than in Case A and Case C. This finding aligns with the importance of experience in biomimicking behaviors. The presence and participation of team members at the time of implementation of self-managed teams are higher in Cases B and C, aligning with the better success of teams in these cases with KPIs.

Self-Managed Teams

The members of the three teams in case studies work as self-managed teams. In Case A, participants described the meaning of working in a self-managed team as relying less on management and raising matters to higher levels only when their support is required. They indicated that the core team members knew what needed to be done as they were the ones to implement it. They described the process of a self-managed team as "two-way communication" and felt that business teams that bring them problems to solve had an "open ear" to hear what the team has to offer.

In Case B, participants described that working in a self-managed team has led their clients to rely on them. They were the ones making the decisions, and in doing that, they had "a lot of leeway to choose what to do." This autonomy provided them the power to provide their viewpoint when needed.

Table 7.5 Description of success of the self-managed team per case

	Success
Case A	Very high
Case B	High
Case C	Perfect

In Case C, participants indicated that they decided on how to approach a problem. Members of self-managed teams know what needs to be done, and they can make key decisions on matters. One participant pointed out that "we have certain targets to meet, so we cannot be fully self-managed, comparing what we have heard about freedom of teams in Google." In general, they indicated that their input is considered valuable, and with the autonomy they have in the team, they enjoy solving problems within the scope of their responsibilities. Evaluation of participants on the success of self-managed teams is shown in Table 7.5.

On the benefits sub-theme of working in self-managed teams and making better decisions, all participants in Case A indicated better decision-making due to autonomy, expert decisions, and diversity of ideas. The team members mentioned "managing ourselves," "not being micromanaged," and "autonomy to solve problems" as benefits of decision-making. The majority of participants in Case B described better decision-making in their self-managed team setting as a benefit, with "no micromanagement," "autonomy to achieve goals," and decisions "coming from people closest to the problem" as their reasons for improvements in decisions.

Improvements in decisions were mentioned by most of the participants in Case C, with "transparency," "seeing the big picture," and "reason for why something needs to be done with a problem" as contributing feedback to the value of higher visibility leading to better decisions.

On efficiency benefits, most of the participants in all cases regarded less overhead, faster, and better outcomes to their team's efficiency. This was the same for personal benefits, with participants describing higher motivation, satisfaction, higher retention, and personal growth as the personal benefits of self-managed teams. Finally, on teamwork, less than half of Cases A and B, and all of the participants in Case C, related to trust, better teamwork, and more engagement resulting from working in self-managed teams. More engagement was prominent in feedback from Case C, but in Case A, all the feedback in the category and most of the participants in the team related to trust as the key teamwork dynamic.

Having a self-managed team setup was not all perfect. Participants indicated various drawbacks in each case, including communication, cross-team work, implementation, and interpersonal issues. These were prominent in Case A, then in Case B, and least in Case C.

In an intelligent swarm, a key attribute is the participation of all members. Participants from Case A indicated they could make better decisions because of their autonomy in the self-managed team. They indicated that they are the experts on the matter, so they are better positioned to make the best possible decisions. They also referred to the diversity of ideas because of the participation of everyone. In Cases B and C, autonomy and decision-making by experts were prominent feedback points. Participants in Case C also liked the overview they had on why they were solving a particular problem, which positioned them to make better decisions. They linked their decisions to customers and facts more than other teams.

On efficiency, team members from Case A indicated less overhead and faster and better outcomes. In Case B, team members described achieving higher quality, which had led to better products. In Case C, the team members put a lot of emphasis on having less overhead and faster processes. Working as a team in a self-managed style also has teamwork benefits. For team members in Case A, the emphasis was on trust, whereas in Cases B and C, they described benefiting from more engagement and better teamwork. From a personal perspective, a higher level of satisfaction and motivation were the benefits of working in a self-managed team in Case A. This feedback was the same in the B and C cases, but they also mentioned personal growth and higher retention. Overall, all three teams participating in the study expressed value in the participation of all team members, although teams in Cases B and C had more positive feedback on this topic.

Core Process

The following sections review the core team process based on how participants described the factors of goal alignment, collaboration, and task (changes and revising tasks as the changes happen).

Goals: Goals and objectives of projects get communicated to the teams as input to their work process. In Case A, participants pointed out that goals are presented to them by the product owner in the form of business requirements or problems. They have team meetings to understand their goals. As a result, before the work gets started, "everyone gets the collective goal." In Case B, participants understood that through a series of meetings, they get general problems or specific feature requirements that align with "strategic focus." Team members in Case B pointed out different layers of goals as their input, from a business problem to design mockups and user stories, indicating a structured breakdown of problems as they progress through the process. In Case C, team members were extremely focused on customer problems and customer feedback while considering metrics such as the budget.

At a high level, all teams in the three cases of the study have some understanding of overall goals and objectives. Team members in Case A followed the process with no specific focus. In Case B, team members had a more structured approach to transforming goals into smaller objectives, from business goals to user stories. In Case C, team members placed a high value on understanding goals from the customer's perspective and achieved customer satisfaction by setting and managing customer expectations.

Task: Intelligent swarms respond to change collectively. Team members in the research work together to address the required changes. Responding to customer problems is the key function that they transform into changes in the products they maintain. Team members in Case A use a focused approach to resolving issues and making changes. They discuss changes in the context of responsibilities, delivery mechanisms, and unblocking the work for a teammate. In Case B, team members discuss a wider range of issues, including refining estimates, what needs to be done by whom, how to get things done better, the work process, and how they may even switch tasks between team members to make things go smoother. In Case C, team members mentioned how they follow the process, work on one topic at a time, and prioritize "low-hanging fruits."

Plan: Planning for work is part of the team process. Participating team members perform activities such as estimating, documenting details, and planning to agree between the team members and the company on how, when, and what to deliver. Results from interviews showed that the team members in Cases A and C engage in planning activities less than in Case B. Team members in Case B also engage in preplanning activities that allow them to be better prepared and aligned for the plan execution.

Alignment and Collaboration: Alignment is related to indications of team members relying on each other, accepting responsibilities together, and trusting each other at the team level. In Case A, team members indicated that trust, responsibility, and general agreement were their team alignment attributes. In Case B, team members had more emphasis on responsibility and a sense of ownership. In Case C, besides responsibility, members referred to team dynamics with phrases like "we are on the same page" and "the team works very well together."

Collaboration within the team happens in team processes like decision-making. Team members in Case B indicated less need for facilitation of discussions. Meetings and facilitation sessions were prominent topics brought up by team members from Cases A and C. In a self-managed team, where team members do many traditional activities associated with the manager, various activities may need team members' facilitation. Members in all of the teams frequently mentioned how they collaborated with external teams and their customer base by demonstrating their work as they informed them, provided updates, got feedback, and established alignment. In this aspect, team members in Case C indicated more frequent collaboration with external teams and customer base.

Knowledge, Share, and Learn: All the teams in the study follow the same review and learning process. After each delivery period, which could be as short as two weeks, team members meet with a wider audience that includes representatives of related teams like architects and product owners, to see how the past period went by, what was good and must be repeated, what had a negative impact and should be avoided, and, in general, what can be learned from the past experience. This approach is the overall structure of all such traditional retrospective meetings, but in these cases, the leadership team has created a culture of acceptance of failure and tolerance of the opinions of others. As a result, everyone participates in the retrospectives, with the facilitator of the meeting going to everyone and asking for their input. It is well understood that this is how the team learns.

Communications Process

Each team in a different company may use different approaches for communication. In the cases in the research and on the frequency of communication, members of Case A have formal meetings to communicate about their work daily. In Case B, team members meet daily but also have weekly meetings to sum up their communication. In Case C, meetings are held twice weekly or weekly. Overall, the team in Case B has more frequent and structured meetings for communication than the teams in Case A and C, and the team in Case C has the lowest frequency of meetings.

Teams use various tools to communicate, including electronic/website boards, direct communications such as meetings, face-to-face discussions, and instant messaging software. They all use the same toolsets that allow them to have direct, passive (people make information available on a channel or website), and visual (a physical or electronic board) communications consistently across all teams.

All the team members from the teams in the three cases of this research use communication as an integral part of their work. They all described the value of communication in different forms. Team members from Case A see communication as a way to inform all team members and provide an opportunity for everyone to participate, ask questions, get feedback, and make progress. For the team in Case B, communication value establishes a cadence for sharing information and alignment. For the team in Case C, communication provides the best visibility and a mechanism to correct any misunderstandings earlier in the process. These are not different views but reflect on internal team dynamics and importance to the team members.

Feedback from participants showed that the roles were clearly defined, with some emphasizing the importance of this clarity as "luckily" and "fortunately." In all cases, team members pointed out that they had multiple roles within the team. Using clear roles, responsibilities, and expectations will be clear too. In total, participants mentioned 15 unique roles. One noticeable indicator I considered was how many unique roles there were and how strongly participants felt about them. This information indicates communication breadth, leading to better communication between the team members of the same team and across different teams. A summary of findings from the feedback was that team members in A and C do more communication and interaction with other roles, both internally and externally.

Decision Process

Intelligent swarms follow six distinct behaviors to make decisions. The following sections review the observed behavior in team members of each team in applying strategies for making decisions. After that, I will present the challenges that team members encountered when making decisions and strategies to resolve the challenges.

Breakdown: If a decision is about a large project or if there are unknowns about various aspects of the decision, members of intelligent swarms break it down into smaller parts so that they can manage each separate part before making a decision. All three teams in the research follow this pattern. Team members in Case A do this breakdown to identify the key parts to understand user stories associated with each part. They may decide to create separate work packages and even complete the work in multiple cycles. The breakdown happens less frequently for team members in Case B. They break the customer problems into subproblems and decide when to do each subproblem. As indicated by one member, they "divide and conquer." In Case C, team members decide to "go one step down" if they face a large problem to solve. They may consult with a senior member to help them break it down into smaller components.

Subgroup: If team members are trying to decide about a problem with too many unknowns, they may divide the team into subgroups to develop different approaches. In the team of Case A, this could be due to insufficient information. Based on their roles, they divide to do some investigation and regroup to present options. In Case B, team members solve this by defining tasks for subgroups or discussing them informally with other teams. They come back to the team-level discussion to develop designs and use visualization approaches like creating mockups to present their findings. Team members in Case C rely on other team members or domain experts. Each person researches or simply asks external stakeholders like architects to help them with the direction. In short, Case A and C team members ask the domain experts for help, which constitutes subgroups with extensions to the team members outside the core team, but in Case B, team members try to learn with internal subgroups and only reach out to external stakeholders on a consulting basis.

Discover Options: This is perhaps one of the most important aspects of intelligent swarms that matter to teamwork. In this pattern, members try to find all the viable options available to them. It is based on discovering viable options, investigating, prototyping, and establishing supportive mechanisms for more feedback. Team members use their knowledge, education, and experience to find viable options. They may do some investigation to come up with options.

The whole team or team members may be tasked to do a prototype to see if an idea is a viable option. They may benefit from structured aids such as a design sketching session. Members of the teams in all three cases in the research use these approaches to discover options. In Case A, team members mostly brainstorm and help to visualize the discussion in sketching sessions. In a sketching session, team members draw their ideas on paper or on the board (physical or electronic) and generate solutions. In Case B, team members also do sketches. They are encouraged to come up with as many ideas as possible, "no matter how crazy." Team members participate in short discovery rounds: they are given a few minutes to ponder the topic, come up with as many solutions as possible, and then present them in one minute. This process helps discover numerous solutions and avoids the attachment of people to a single idea because they have had a short time to invest in it. Team members in Case C use sketches and short discovery rounds, research their competitors' designs to see what they can learn, and may even reach out to the customer base to get more ideas.

Discuss Options: We do not necessarily see a discussion, not at least in the human version of it in intelligent swarms. What we have observed, and I have elaborated on in the previous chapters, is observed in various species like bees through behaviors like flying in a particular flight dance. In teamwork, team members discuss options to understand and improve the possible solutions. Each team benefits from different techniques. Team members in Case A use whiteboards, open discussion, brainstorming, fact-based reasoning, and a score to prioritize based on the combination of the number of customers affected, confidence in the solution, impact, and effort.

The discussion between team members in Case B is also in free form and based on evaluating the complexity of options, minimum viable product, and value-adding capability of the options. In Case C, team members also benefit from brainstorming and whiteboarding, but they rely on role-based recommendations rather than team-level discussions and voting.

Opine: Though discreet, intelligent swarms do not impose any limitations on their members. Each one can warn, call, and become a source of information that the whole swarm utilizes in response to a situation. This is different if a dominant member is more vocal and/or has been bestowed authority to drive decisions. In teamwork, after discovering options, self-managed team members participate in activities that lead to choosing the desired option or making a decision. The process is simple as the team's size is small, so a quick vote usually works. However, members of teams in the research use various tools and techniques to ensure everyone's input and participation.

Team members of the team in Case A try to get to a consensus, but they use voting if there are any doubts. They use online tools and post polls so everyone can go and vote. Voting is done anonymously, so the act of voting does not influence people. If the decision is about selecting a few items among a larger number of options, they each get 3–5 votes, which they can "spend" on one or more options.

In Case B, voting is not as common as the team discusses various options to get to a consensus. Team members may apply the same multiple-vote method when they can have more than one outcome. Team members in Case C are encouraged to participate in the discussions by the facilitators. They vote on options using online tools. There is an emphasis on the "people weighing in" and "democratic" approach. The team members leave decisions to the expertise of each role and only vote on items that can affect everyone.

Strengthen decision: Agents/members of an intelligent swarm are quick to respond to various situations. For example, in case of danger, they start imitating the warning sound immediately. Implementing a self-managed team encourages the team members to participate in the decision-making process without the fear of failure. The process devised by leaders in teams involved in my research has a corrective mechanism in the form of retrospective discussions that happen every two weeks. Team members review and discuss how they did over the last working period and learn together as a team.

Team members in Case A mentioned various review points, including design review and code review. They de-risk the design decisions by trying them early in the process to revise their decision if they need to. In Case B, team members have the same review points. To de-risk, they do rapid prototyping and hold a demo session to show their work and the decisions they have made and to get early feedback. In Case C, team members may decide to run a Proof of Concept (PoC) on large decisions to see which option works better. Developing a PoC may not be possible due to time and cost factors.

Overcome Decision-Making Challenges: Self-managed team implementation should provide methods for decision-making. Compared to traditional team management methods, team members should have methods to overcome similar challenges without the constant support of a manager. During data collection, team members of all teams brought up various issues and the solutions they had in place if the challenges arose.

In the categorization of issues, I concluded two different themes for these challenges: personal and technical. Personal challenges arise from team members' disagreements, groupthink, attachment to personal views, and refusal to participate. On the technical side, challenges include dependency on other teams (i.e., for them to do something so work can continue on this team), missing information or solutions, and dealing with major changes.

Regardless of the type of challenge, team members try to overcome it by collecting data (gathering information, consulting, getting direct feedback) and working as a team (team advocacy, aligning on dependencies, learning as a team). In the following sections, I review how team members of each team deal with these challenges.

Team members in Case A described a variety of challenges that they encountered and had to resolve. On the personal side, if there is a disagreement between team members, they ask for supporting data. By reflecting on facts instead of emotions, they reach a logical conclusion using reasoning. They may decide to consult with more experienced stakeholders outside of the team, such as architects. If the disagreement is on estimations, they work as a team and discuss further to bring their estimates closer and go with a higher number to avoid underestimations. To avoid personal attachment to a solution, they hold ideation sessions, providing a short time for members to develop solutions. Having spent a very small amount of time, team members do not get attached to the ideas and evaluate all suggestions equally.

On technical challenges, team members in Case A collaborate and backtrack to find which decision led to the situation if something is not working. Suppose there is missing information or they do not have a solution to a problem. In that case, they collect the data and investigate the solution (this pattern was reviewed earlier in the "Subgroup" and "Discover Options" sections). If the change is major, they approach the decision with more investigation and discussion and may consult with other stakeholders, such as a product owner, outside of the team. In some cases, the team members may vote for direct customer feedback. They can "hire" customer groups to participate in their discussion and even be part of their pilot runs to come up with the best decision.

Team members in Case B did not describe any personal challenges. Still, on the technical side, if there are dependencies, they try to coordinate with external teams. If there are delays, they postpone decisions/work on the topics until clarity is provided. If something goes wrong, they review it retrospectively to avoid it in the future. If there are specific scenarios or "edge cases," they document them and work to get the missing information.

In Case C, team members described dealing with disruptive team members by asking them to back up their ideas using data. They mentioned allowing team members to opine on their fields of expertise, but they asked all team members to comply with majority votes, even if it meant a failure point, and they would have to reverse the decision. They advocate working as a team and even failing as a team, as it is not seen as a failure but a learning opportunity, or, as a team member described, "live and learn." The team has experienced cases in which they could not decide between two opposing ideas. In those situations, they decide based on a–b testing, a method with a small population of end users who see two different product versions. The team members track each option's success to extend the better solution to all customers, allowing customers' actual preferences to be the final decision-making factor.

SUMMARY

This chapter presented a detailed analysis of the descriptive multiple case study to answer the research question: What are the common decision-making strategies for self-managed teams as experienced by team members using behaviors exhibited in intelligent swarms? The responses from team members were categorized into six main categories: experience, role, Self-Managed Team (SMT), team process, communications, and decision. Categories were then structured to lead to factors and themes. These factors were mapped to behaviors identified in previous chapters containing observations in intelligent swarms.

I provided a summary of these behaviors and the evidence of applying similar patterns in self-managed teams in each case, with some variances as they each have adopted approaches that work best with their environment. I also analyzed and summarized the key performance indicators that the leaders of the participating company track to measure each team's success. Findings showed that all behaviors of biomimicking could be observed in how teams in the study work. The next chapter consists of an in-depth interpretation of the study's findings, along with potential limitations and generalizations.

Chapter 8

Research Results and Conclusions

The purpose of the research was to see if teams that functioned in a self-managed setup were utilizing similar behaviors like intelligent swarms, and if so, were they able to produce better results? The selection of multiple cases from the same company allowed the elimination of unequal parameters such as general team setup, leadership support, budgets, products, markets, and so on. The choice of market, that is, technology industry, allowed for fast-paced changes, not exactly how fast nature presents challenges to its inhabitants but as close as it can get in a working environment setting.

Having multiple teams in the research allowed the triangulation of minor differences, opportunities, and challenges in work processes, team dynamics, and behaviors. It showed that the implementation of self-managed principles was perceived slightly differently, which allowed further niche results to be extrapolated by juxtaposing the behaviors and achieving the goals.

I wanted to see what mattered in the implementation of a self-managed team so I could present a new team setup for an Intelligent Team at the end. In my research for this valuable setup, I noticed gaps in team setup in all the companies that I approached and non-conclusive guidance from the academic world. Most of the companies focus on the functions, products, and goals and try to match the expertise of members with those. However, as I've shown so far, that's just the basic structure of team building.

The self-managed setting, which comes closest to enabling team members to be the best they can be, is even poorer than traditional methods, on both commercial and academic sides. They all cover parts of the problems and challenges that such teams may face. For example, back in 2017, researchers Liff and Gustavson provided high-level guidelines for self-managed team implementation but did not address the decision-making approach and implementation challenges.

The unique perspective that I brought into this mix was what we might be able to do by biomimicking intelligent swarms. It provides a wide range of behaviors for team members to follow. The key idea behind this is the similarity between the autonomy of self-managed teams and the behaviors exhibited by social beings in intelligent swarms, applicable in various teamwork activities such as decision-making.

DOI: 10.1201/9781003527206-11

Findings from the analysis of collected data show that biomimicking and learning from intelligent swarms can provide appropriate guidelines for implementing successful self-managed teams. All nine behaviors for general work processes and six behaviors of decision-making considered from biomimicking exist in implementing self-managed teams in the research. However, as mentioned earlier, slight differences and variances in approaches taken by each team provided great input to solidify the principles and guidelines for building Intelligent teams.

WHAT DO FINDINGS TEACH US?

Going in, we knew that for the successful implementation of self-managed teams, organizations should go through a transformation that can enable team members to use the autonomy they have in a self-managed approach and work effectively. Back in 2015, researchers started looking into further applications of biomimicking and swarm intelligence in computing, image processing, logistics, and other innovative solutions (Ismail et al., 2015). The idea of biomimicking as a source of innovation for management came to me from there, especially as I was working with IT teams that were working independently to a great degree. If we could run teams the same way that intelligent swarms produced a new level of behavior, why not connect the two and see what we might learn? I investigated the potential benefits of understanding group behavior between humans and social beings in the context of self-managed teams.

Based on a conceptual framework consisting of teamwork, decision-making, and sociobiology constructs, I considered elements of self-management using self-determination theory, social learning theory, and social choice theory. All these should help with a solid implementation of self-managed teams that can guide leadership, communications, and decision-making to avoid challenges that lower performance. I call this unique implementation an Intelligent Team.

The fundamental difference between self-managed and traditional teams is the autonomy in making decisions. To efficiently enable a self-managed team, team members need to address challenges such as polarization and groupthink, low synergy, and weaknesses in team cohesion. My research extended the application of intelligent swarms to self-managed teams using the same simple rules that social beings exhibit by showing how team members apply decision-making strategies and other behaviors.

The learnings from social beings provided nine behaviors for teamwork and communication processes. For the decision process, six behaviors were mapped to decision patterns. In the following sections, I review the findings and provide interpretations based on participants' feedback and the company's KPIs.

Experience

Experience plays a key role in any work situation. Working as a team is related to team dynamics and teamwork collaborations. The results of the research showed that teams who had experience with self-managed setups did better in meeting their KPIs. In other words, if companies are setting up a new self-managed team and ultimately invest in an Intelligent Team with the proper setup I am going to show in the final chapter, they can expect improved performance as team members gain experience working within the new settings.

The other point worth mentioning is that experience in all forms helps. Teams that can do a better job of collaborating with businesses and aligning with their goals will have better fulfillment of business requirements.

Self-Managed Team

Comparing the benefits feedback across the three cases shows similar decision-making improvements, but there are differences in how much efficiency is gained by each team. This difference comes from the consideration of the personal value of the setting, which points to a realization that team members believe that self-managed settings are better than traditional settings. As such, part of the plan to transition teams to become Intelligent Teams will have to include training, not just on the setup but also on showing how the setting can be better for each team member, for the team, and for the organization overall.

An important construct of a self-managed setting is full participation by all team members. The concept of swarm intelligence for a team is only possible when all members participate in the same way it materializes in nature. Goals are, of course, different, but the concepts are transferable.

Absolute participation is a more complex problem for team members due to differences in personalities and other options available to them. However, the implementation of a self-managed setting creates a level of autonomy and freehand in decision-making to the degree that they are motivated, engaged, and want to stay and contribute. Observations showed that in teams with a higher participation rate, there is a higher sense of belonging and being valued, which led to a higher sense of success in the context of a self-managed setting.

This was a major contributor to teams either meeting their KPIs or working with the customers to set the right expectations and achieve customer satisfaction in the process.

On the personal side, all team members across the three cases indicated they are satisfied with their work and motivated to do better as a result. Members from Cases B and C also mentioned they were growing at a personal level, and they have observed much higher employee retention as a result. Team members in Case A have more issues and drawbacks than those in Cases B and C, confirming more successful outcomes for those teams. Team members in Cases B and C showed higher participation, which is a key biomimicking behavior, aligning with and confirming the confluence of the emerged research pattern and biomimicking behavior.

Core Process

The core process of teamwork includes elements required for performing the jobs of the team and the output expected of the team. Tuckman's team-building stages still apply: People are put together to form a team. They storm, discuss how to approach things, and reach a norming stage. Norms eventually become what teams need to do, and the team starts performing.

On awareness of goals and responding to changes, teams in all three cases follow the biomimicking behavior of understanding the goals with a slight difference in using them within their process. There is no KPI for understanding the goals. Team members in Case A focus on their current goal. When a change happens, they must redirect their efforts to handle the change because there is no support mechanism. This finding aligns with performance results for Case A, as they do not fully meet the business goals and customer satisfaction due to a lack of provisioning for customer support and change management. In Case B, team members have a structured approach to goals as they break them down from overall goals to user stories that they work on, and at the same time, they monitor a wide range of changes. Team members in Case B meet the business goals and customer satisfaction KPIs. In Case C, team members have the same challenge of changing and redirecting their resources, but they focus on customer needs and constantly consider delivering value to customers. As a result, they exceed customer satisfaction and meet business goals.

The lack of incorporating larger goals for the team in Case A led team members to be more focused on solving more immediate problems and disconnecting from larger-scale changes. Members of intelligent swarms respond to change collectively while moving toward the overall goal. Missing delivery dates and claim-to-commit milestones are symptoms of this lack of focus for the team in Case A. Team members in Case B follow the process closely and show more flexibility in switching tasks between themselves to keep the goals of the projects intact. As a result, they meet their delivery dates regularly and normally exceed their Claim-to-Commit KPI (meaning they deliver more than they commit). Team members in Case C work on one item at a time and give priority to easier items. As such, they may not give enough priority to more important items, which is why they miss their delivery and commitment KPIs.

The planning factor is another consideration in team management, with special differences in self-management settings. The results of the data analysis indicated that team members in Case B do more planning and engage in preplanning activities. Biomimicking behavior from intelligent swarms indicates the importance of understanding the plan by everyone, especially when there is an emergency change. Although all teams engage in planning activities, a higher level of engagement indicated by participants in Case B and the preplanning activity has helped the team do better in achieving KPIs of delivery dates and claim-to-commit.

Alignment and collaboration elements are directly related to teamwork and contribute to team dynamics and how the team will be able to go through various stages of Tuckman's model. Alignment and collaboration are two of the traditional team constructs, but a self-managed team should be implemented so that these functions can work without the supervision of a manager. Most of the team's input consists of goals and objectives. These get communicated to the teams in the study in the form of customer problems.

The implementation of a self-managed team in the participating company makes it clear that the responsibility of solving the problem is with the team members. Once the problem is understood within the context of the team, team members commit to delivering the solution to the problem. That commitment and responsibility are understood across the three teams in the research. Besides the responsibility, participants in Case A indicated a strong sense of trust between team members. They work with each other to get to an agreement. In other cases, there are team dynamics such as a sense of ownership and cohesiveness, so team members work together to come up with solutions, plans, and delivery.

Collaboration happens through various communication forms, but in essence, team members gather in a physical or virtual room to discuss the problem. A major difference between traditional teams and self-managed teams is facilitation. At each stage of problem-solving, a lead role facilitates discussions. This feedback to other team members and playing the facilitator's role aligns with similar behaviors in intelligent swarms, with members closer to the external change initiating the call to action.

The learning factor in a team is a key construct related to social learning theory. On learning, all the teams in the study follow the review and retrospective processes and meet after each work cycle to review how they did and evaluate their performance. This approach aligns with the biomimicking behaviors of learning lessons from experience.

Communications Process

Communication is the underlying theme in many aspects of conceptual and practical teamwork effort and the root of success in many of the processes, enabling accomplishing tasks to go beyond each team member and toward a team as a unit. In communications, constant sharing of status and information is a repeating biomimicking behavior. Members of intelligent swarms constantly monitor their surroundings and react to changes. Others follow a change initiated, and as a result, swarm behavior appears. In the view of team members, communications happen for reasons such as sharing, participating, establishing a cadence, visibility, and de-risking. Case B had the highest frequency of official communication points between the three cases in the research, and Case C had the least. There are different levels and contents to communicate for different reasons. One of them is when team members communicate across different roles within the team. Cases A and C did this more often, but instead, in Case B, members were more focused and did more frequent communication, which helped them meet business goals and customer satisfaction.

In Cases A and C, the wider range of roles means they must work with more people, showing that their type of work requires having more communication points, leading to missing information and some business goals. Team members in Case C exceed customer expectations, which can be interpreted as a customer-oriented mindset, as they give priority to visible issues to customers but miss other goals.

In conclusion, teamwork and communication processes, a closer implementation, and the following of biomimicking behaviors have led to more team success. Team members in Case B match with more of these behaviors, and they succeeded in meeting all their KPIs and exceeding a few. Team members in Case C focus on customers and have been establishing processes that help them achieve business goals and customer satisfaction KPIs but only partially meet delivery and commit-to-claim. They can increase their planning efforts, change management, responsiveness, and internal communications to overcome their challenges. This approach applies to team members in Case A, but they also have to increase their external communications and manage expectations.

Decision Process

Autonomy to make teamwork-related decisions is a fundamental attribute of a self-managed setting. This also happens to be the most significant feature of intelligent swarms that can make decisions fast and effectively by applying their learned instincts, which are learned processes perfected over millions of years.

The decision process consists of breaking down a large decision into smaller ones, subgroups to understand all aspects, discovering as many options as possible, discussing the options, participating in discussions and opining, making decisions, and strengthening them through reviews and learning. Not all of these components may be done on the same decision depending on how much team members know about it, if there is missing information, or if the team has made similar decisions before. The following sections provide an interpretation of findings on these components of the decision-making process. All aspects of the decision process tie back to decision theory and social choice theory as team members share their thoughts and experiences in the form of options to make decisions, as well as teamwork theory as the team members review available paths to solve a challenge while going through various stages of team building toward the normalization stage of the Tuckman model.

Team members in Cases A and C indicated that they encountered decisions that they had to break down into smaller pieces more than members in Case B. This difference is because team members in Case B do this by transforming goals into smaller steps, and when it is time to decide, they already have user stories to look at instead of a big unknown problem. If they have a bigger problem to solve, they bring it up in their daily meeting, and the whole team participates in the discussion. In Case A, breakdowns happen internally, whereas in Case C, they consult with external stakeholders. Regarding dividing teams into subgroups, all teams in the three cases subgroup to discover missing information, but the difference is that in Cases A and C, this is done by role, meaning that the team members with specific roles, like developer or designer, take a problem away and try to solve it; however in Case B, team members discuss it at the team level.

On discovery of options, all the teams in the research perform sketching sessions to help them visualize what the results should resemble. They brainstorm and engage in short round sessions that help them come up with many ideas in a short time. In Case C, team members perform an extra step and check the competitors' designs to see how they can learn from them.

On discussing and opining on options, all teams have free-form conversations as they review aspects of what they need to decide. These discussions are facilitated by one of the team members, depending on where on the process the team is. For example, in the beginning, the product owner facilitates the discussion while communicating the customer's problem. After that, a system analyst or business analyst will facilitate so team members can develop an approach. Next, a designer will facilitate so they can come up with design ideas.

In many cases, team members reach a consensus, and there is no need for voting. Team members in Cases A and B use a simple voting method to choose one option. If they can choose more than one item (for example, they can start working on three user stories and want to vote for the priority among the next ten items), then they use a multi-vote method. Using an online tool or a whiteboard, team members get two or three votes, and they spend their votes on what they think matters most. Team members in Case C give priority to the roles in voting. For example, it is up to a designer to choose a design unless they want to consult with the team.

In Case A, team members encounter personal challenges like disagreements and attachment to one's ideas. They have methods to encounter each type of issue. On the technical side, if there is missing information, they collect it from the input source, such as the business unit lead or customers. Team members in Case B have been able to resolve their personal challenges in the decision-making process, so they remain focused on technical aspects. They ask each other to support the claims with data, and if there is missing information, they strive to find out. In Case C, team members also look for data to support discussions. When making hard decisions, they try to de-risk it by running it to fail or succeed as early as possible so they have time to correct it. These slight differences in Cases A, B, and C have led to different KPI results. In Case A, many of the KPIs are missed because they do not prepare for emergencies and have to overcome personal challenges in the decision-making process. In Case B, they do not miss on external changes and are ready for them. They do pre-planning, which helps them be more realistic about their commitments, and they have already figured out how to work as a team. This approach can be related to their experience as the most mature self-managed team across the three cases in the study. In Case C, team members face similar problems as Case A, but their approach to finding drawbacks of their decisions sooner and closer collaboration with customers gives them an advantage on business and customer satisfaction KPIs, even though they miss delivery dates and claim-to-commit indicators.

LIMITATIONS OF THE RESEARCH

Every research has limitations on how much it'd be able to cover of reality of the situation under investigation. This one is not an exception. As far as I am aware, this research was its first kind for trying to investigate a link between intelligent swarms and the management of teams, hence limited on what could be relied on and backed by previous works.

Also, the nature of the research through case studies makes it generally limited to very similar situations. However, I've made sure to eliminate the underlying industry in my approach, which makes it easy to generalize the findings and recommendations. Throughout this chapter and the one before, I constantly showed how the research is based on well-established concepts and theories, and no conflicting results came out throughout the research.

RECOMMENDATIONS

This study was the first of its kind in the interdisciplinary field of self-management and sociobiology. The findings showed an alignment between successful self-managed settings and practices with intelligent swarm behaviors, which open a whole new field and future research possibilities.

Like any research, this one started with a passion for seeking the possibility of learning from nature. History is full of lessons humans have learned from observing nature and even the behavior of social beings. The question at the beginning of the journey of the research was to see how we can learn from the behavior of social beings in management. Like all other research, I had to go through a long process to narrow down the scope of the research to be able to achieve the quality required to establish proper relationships. That is now done, and a whole new field is open for further research.

Implementation of self-managed teams varies across different companies as it depends on many different factors, including decisions on decentralization, level of self-management, and applying required changes. For that reason, scholars have either provided high-level guidelines or elaborated on particular areas of interest in self-managed team implementation, like leadership style or success of the method. This research and method devised in the final chapters set a new source of simplifying the variances that the organization's leaders will have to decide when implementing a self-managed team toward a new level of team functionality and success by following behaviors exhibited in intelligent swarms or, as I have called it, an Intelligent Team.

The Intelligent Team approach provides insights into other processes of teams, such as communications, collaboration, and alignment. Future research should consider studies with a focus on other processes, including elements of team dynamics like trust or cohesiveness of team members.

The background and experience of organizational leaders can be a major factor in the implementation of self-managed teams. One finding in the research was that groupthink was a challenge in discussion but no more than traditionally managed teams. Team members pointed out that dealing with specific problems such as groupthink requires responsible leaders for the implementation of self-managed teams to be familiar with this issue and provide avoidance processes for it; however, many of these leaders may not have the background to know its effects as they normally rise in ranks from technical/work/functional backgrounds. Future research on leaders' backgrounds and experiences who implement self-managed teams may provide insights into this matter.

New biomimicking behaviors may help extend the recommendations for the implementation of self-managed teams. Seeley (2010) started his research on the honeybee decision-making process years before new video technology enabled him to find the underlying approach bees follow for making decisions and how they move the colony toward the new nest. Field researchers will continue to discover new behaviors that may be useful for self-managed teams or other aspects of management.

We learned from the research that intelligent swarm behaviors were constantly present and following them helped to improve the successful outcomes of self-managed teams. It was also shown that following biomimicking behaviors by members of self-managed teams improves their work experience and outcome.

Going back a level higher, we can see that by establishing intelligent swarms' behaviors as a source for successful team behaviors, a logical relationship has been established between the principles of social-determination theory, social learning theory, and social choice theory from one side, and behavioral learnings from Wilson's sociobiology constructs.

The results contribute to the social determination theory on how team members are motivated to participate and benefit from the autonomy they have in the implementation of self-managed teams. It strengthens social choice theory in reaching consensus in self-managed teams and de-risking the decisions by being open to revising if needed when the early results of feedback become available.

Positive Effect at All Levels

Before I close this chapter, I'd like to emphasize the people-side value of Intelligent Teams. Nowadays, it may be really hard to find ways to motivate your employees and gain their loyalty. A high percentage of participants mentioned satisfaction, personal growth, loyalty, and high motivation because of their team setup. The closer the team was following intelligent swarm behaviors, the higher positive personal feelings toward the job, resulting in higher retention, consistently meeting KPIs, and, in general, happier employees. This resembles the kernel of a positive social change.

More success and consistency in teams that follow biomimicking behaviors will enable team members to manage challenges, collaborate within the team and outside of the team with other business units and customers, speculate the upcoming changes, and organize more effectively.

Here is another good news: Implementation of Intelligent Team using biomimicking behaviors is simple, such as the behavior of social beings that inspired them. These achievements may stimulate leaders of other teams within the organization or other organizations to implement biomimicking self-managed teams. Achieving more goals and objectives will enable organizational leaders to align resources better, amplify organizational and personal achievements, and may lead to positive social change.

At a personal level, satisfaction and growth will lead to a healthier state of mind for team members, inspire more work innovations, and contribute to better work-life balance. This state will have positive effects on the larger scale of families and society. At the organizational level, having a simpler and more successful approach to implementing a self-managed team will inspire more leaders to adopt such teams in their organizations.

From an educational view, I hope this research and this book inspire business schools to consider a new perspective in management practices supported by nature and provide organizations with new methods to manage complicated situations using simple rules of biomimicking and intelligent swarms' behaviors. This awareness will allow institutionalizing the approach as an advanced yet simple method of setting teams and organizations for success.

What Comes Next

With the positive results of the research demonstrated in the last two chapters, I am ready to take you to the final step of this journey. I am going to provide a toolkit to build your own Intelligent Team. This will be done through providing tools for implementing such team, including training and allowing the required thought process in organizational leaders, choosing the right structures for the Intelligent Teams, providing them with the strategy and vision they need to thrive within, training the team members how to function as such team, establish new values aligned with intelligent swarms behaviors that have proven useful in building success, and other tools for primary functions like decision-making and building team dynamics among others.

Part 4

Intelligent Team Toolkit

In Part 4, I am going to provide a toolkit for teams and leaders who wish to build a successful, Intelligent Team. I will start with a short recap, followed by the principles that we learned from the similarities between intelligent swarms and teamwork. I will then move to a few short chapters that provide more details, and where appropriate, I provide step-by-step guidance for building Intelligent Teams from various aspects, along with more examples of intelligent swarms' behavior. The physical form of the toolkit, containing tools for decision-making workshops and various forms of voting, is available at www.intelligentteam.ca.

Our ultimate goal is to have a practical approach to building an Intelligent Team. This concept is unique; however, there are good models and approaches out there that are worth mentioning. One, called a High-Performance Team (HPT) proposed as a team leadership model by Ginnett (documented in their book, Hughes et al., 2009). An HPT has three goals: providing acceptable outcomes to stakeholders, achieving satisfaction by team members, and improving the future capabilities of the team. Biomimicking through replicating behaviors of intelligent swarms supports all these components, plus lots of extra pointers for practical, guaranteed methods of success taken from social beings.

RECAP OF INTELLIGENT SWARM BEHAVIORS

This is a recap of what we learned from intelligent swarms and a short description of what we are going to do with them:

Bats

Behaviors: Send signals, identify targets, constantly monitor surrounding, Correct course according to movements of targets and other bats

Applications: Set the goal and monitor the current state versus goals. Make information available. Make adjustments to plans as you move forward. Always check to see if a correction is required. Try to narrow down the choices to two for easier decision-making.

Flocks of Birds

Behaviors: Birds follow simple rules to achieve the benefits of looking like a swarm (protection, prey, etc.), like considering the distance from the bird in front and changing direction with them. These behaviors are mapped in particle swarm optimization. Collision is possible (as in people's ideas), and different speeds are welcome (people can get to the same conclusion at their own pace).

Applications: Allow people time to adjust their understanding and change of direction. Maintain different ideas to ensure points of view are not missed.

Schools of Fish

Behaviors: Follow very simple rules like search, swarm, chase, and leap. This is all based on a field of vision.

Applications: Inputs from all team members provide a stronger way of forecasting, better decision-making, and improved planning. The prerequisite is to provide the proper field of vision to team members.

Fireflies

Behaviors: Various intensities and frequencies of signals for mating, warning, or forage purposes. Simplified, the swarm moves toward a brighter one. Work in smaller sub-swarms to circumvent threads and achieve smaller goals.

Applications: Change stance on a decision-making situation based on what others are offering. Establish sub-teams or committees to address a larger number of goals or milestones. Generate alternatives.

Wolves

Behaviors: Separate and search for food. Call out when found. Wolf also packs work based on hierarchy.

Applications: Break into smaller problems and reattach to a larger scope once done. Call out when encountering challenges. Use hierarchy rules to transition the team to self-managed. Team members get to "howl" when they find a new possibility.

Ants

Behaviors: Choice of the shortest path, using different types of pheromones – which last different amounts of time, from 20 minutes to hours or days – to indicate a prey or plant food. Helps to put the overall picture together.

Applications: Use experience to choose the optimum approach. Use lessons learned, organizational knowledge, and personal knowledge. Communicate the experience. Connect all smaller opportunities to get the overall picture.

Honeybees

Behaviors: Communicating sources of food. Decision about new nest and selection process. Process of moving the swarm to the new nest.

Applications: Decision-making, road-mapping, goal-setting, cascade-down goals, leadership.

INTELLIGENT TEAM PRINCIPLES

The behaviors mentioned earlier, based on the research and what we already know about teamwork, led to these principles:

Strategy and Goal Principle: Understand the overall team function, goals, and required tasks.

Collective Response Principle: Respond to internal and external changes collectively.

Emergency Principle: Understand and plan for emergencies.

Teamwork Principle: Understand the equality of all members and feel comfortable opining in team activities.

Watch Principle: Know about end goals and periodically check for internal or external system changes. Team members strive to stay in alignment with other team members. In this way, team members can make small corrections to stay on track.

Member Difference Principle: Understand that, due to different frames of reference, certain team members may need more time to reach the same level of understanding. They should collaborate to reach the same degree of understanding or move in the same direction in thought processes. Team members with closer points of view and those with different ideas should consult with each other frequently.

Information Flow Principle: Iteratively share information and communicate changes.

Knowledge Transfer Principle: Because team members may have different perspectives, members should constantly transfer knowledge to ensure information distribution.

Experience Principle: Consider team members' experience, organizational knowledge, and lessons learned from past tasks and prioritize and validate options presented through experience.

And around decision-making, we learned the following principles:

Problem Breakdown Principle: Break down the problem into smaller sub-problems with few and preferably binary options and discuss the best choice with all team members. Team members will continue to solve other problems until they find a clear solution to the main problem.

Choice Discussion Principle: Communicate alternatives and discuss choices iteratively to reach a stronger acceptance of the decision.

Choice Discovery Principle: Discover and present potential solutions and invite team members to explore solutions. Team members should advocate for the strongest solutions, regardless of who first presented them, checking other solutions with open minds.

Sub-team Principle: Divide into subgroups to find different potential solutions if team members cannot find clear alternatives. Team members exchange subgroups to trigger innovation.

Participation Principle: Opine on selected solutions and change parameters to discover a potentially stronger solution variation.

Ownership Principle: After a decision is made, the team, not the people who perhaps came up with the original idea, own it and should continue to explain the approach to others who do not understand or were not able to take part in the discussions for any reason.

In the next few chapters, I will tie these principles with various elements of building an Intelligent Team Toolkit.

Chapter 9

Setting Up an Intelligent Team – a Change in Mindset and Organization

This chapter summarizes everything that the leaders of the organization will have to do to set up successful Intelligent Teams. The topics were widely discussed across the book, so this is a summary plus a set of actions and recommendations to help leaders implement efficient Intelligent Teams.

EMPOWERMENT

A major component of the Intelligent Team is the change of mindset. Most, if not all, of the people are used to working in some settings, mostly traditional, where a hierarchy defines what they can or cannot do. Unless they carry a management title, they do not make decisions. They simply do what they are told to do, with some freedom on specific tasks they have in hand and how to do it. In many companies, any behavior outside of this is discouraged. In cases where they allow employees to be more adventurous, the discovery and development are mostly done individually and not developed as a team. This is the essential difference between a traditional team and an Intelligent Team.

Therefore, the main function of organizational leadership is empowering the members of Intelligent Teams, so they feel comfortable achieving the true power of their capabilities and, in return, elevate the goals and objectives of the corporate strategy. This may be hard for some leaders as they have to accept reducing their own influence and transition from decision-makers to decision architects. In that role, they provide the blueprints of success, and Intelligent Team members decide how to get there (Figures 9.1 and 9.2).

INSTIGATING FULL ENGAGEMENT

Team members in Intelligent Team get to experience their true strength through full engagement. Full engagement means being an integral part of the team, driving the implementation of strategy, and being part of the decision-making mechanism. I am going to go back to nature for a few more

DOI: 10.1201/9781003527206-13

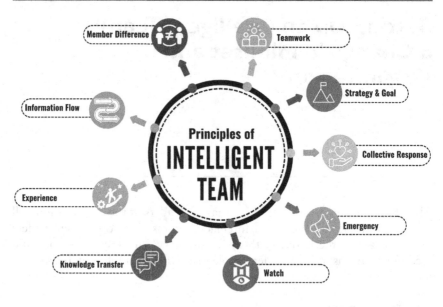

Figure 9.1 The nine principles of building Intelligent Teams

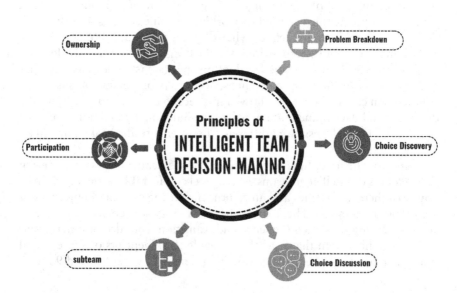

Figure 9.2 The six principles of intelligent team decision-making

inspirations before listing organizational changes that need to be implemented to support Intelligent Teams.

A great story from Intelligent Swarms is about an African termite with the scientific name of *Macrotermes bellicosus*. This type of termite is known to build big nests as tall as 5 meters and contain over 2 million inhabitants.

Figure 9.3 An African termite mound

The nest contains chambers of chewed wood as a substrate for the symbiotic fungus maintained within the nest. This fungus garden is maintained at 30 ± 1 degree Celsius and carbon dioxide concentration of around 2.6% (Figure 9.3).

This amazing construction is not built by the same workforce as it gets reviewed constantly but through constant collaboration. When a segment of the nest is destroyed by elements of nature or predators, the termites close to the affected area start hitting their heads in the tunnels of the nest, a process called head-banging. This sends the signal to others. They pick up a stone and rush toward the sound. After placing the stone on the damaged wall, they join the head-banging. With louder noise, more and more termites bring in building materials and fix the damage or deal with the intrusion.

Up in the skies, starlings fly in their usual loose formation when above a hawk but draw together into a tight flock when the hawk is above them (a formation known as a murmuration). The reason for this is that a hawk needs to strike its prey with its talons first. If it has to do this with a high speed and through a swarm of birds, it is going to risk getting badly injured. It's like driving into a wall! So this simple behavior demonstrates and works at a higher level of intelligence beyond what each starling can achieve (Figure 9.4).

Figure 9.4 A flock of common starlings flying in close proximity, a behavior known as murmuration

Figure 9.5 Newly hatched owl fly larvae forming a defense line

Another group behavior that shows the manifestation of swarm intelligence can be observed in newly hatched owl fly larvae. When confronted by predators coming toward them, they gather together and raise their heads with big jaws and rapidly snap them, defending themselves as a unit (Figure 9.5).

The common denomination in these stories is the need for survival, which has evolved into masterpiece behaviors. For an organization to be the host of Intelligent Teams, the organizational leaders need to understand how to simulate the basic principles elaborated. In empowerment and with full engagement, the team setup emphasizes on true *Teamwork Principle*, planning for exceptions through the *Emergency Principle*, processes to support the effective working of the *Knowledge Transfer Principle*, and ensuring the sharing of information through the *Information Flow Principle*.

MEASURING PERFORMANCE

Intelligent Team is a community, a semi-company on its own. It does need the support of auxiliary functions to be able to perform its duties; however, it is best to identify customer needs (or, in general, the expectations) from the Intelligent Team and let its members come up with a plan of action to meet the said expectations. Priorities can be communicated along with KPIs that suggest the pace. The Intelligent Team will evaluate and adjust itself to align with strategy, priorities, and expectations.

The success of KPIs and achievements can be evaluated on a quarterly based review. That's how much is required for an Intelligent Team to gear up and get to its optimum working state. The team will use an agreed-upon benchmarking tool, as shown in the "Benchmarking" chapter later in this book.

Traditional teams have a manager or a team leader. Intelligent Teams are based on self-managed teams and do not require to be led by a single person. Everyone is in full engagement and a decision-maker. The role of the team leads, or managers will transform into a facilitator. They will focus on removing obstacles for the team and collaborate with the business and the rest of the company to ensure the success of the Intelligent Teams. The bonus is that because they are not constantly needed, they can be the facilitator of more than one team or establish new Intelligent Teams as the company grows.

TEAM BUILDING

We also need to perform skillful team building exercises to make sure the Intelligent Team has all the technical skills, tools, and soft skills to succeed. While we want the team members to feel heard and equal, there are certain skills that certain members will have and others won't. The trust I will elaborate on in the next few segments later will help the Experience Principle to be applied safely without creating a superiority or groupthink situation. Examples of these team-building exercises can be found in the "From Manager/Team Lead to Facilitator" chapter.

TRAIN FACILITATORS

An organization that successfully establishes Intelligent Teams will need fewer managers and team leads. Instead, it will need to have Intelligent Team facilitators who can help establish such teams, train the employees, and play the bridge between Intelligent Teams and the rest of the company. This is covered in more depth in "From Manager/Team Lead to Facilitator." In terms of working with the rest of the company, a good practice is to keep a facilitator to converse with the rest of the teams if many need interactions; otherwise, the whole team can meet up to ensure transparency. The facilitator can do the job for more than one team, so there are some extra savings in that perspective as well.

DE-RISKING DRAWBACKS

Working in a team brings challenges. When someone works alone, they control many more factors of their outcome. It's much more self-reflective. In a team setting, they have to deal with many more elements outside of their immediate control.

Some of these challenges are well documented by textbooks and popular books alike, including lack of trust, conflicts, and lack of commitment, among others. While these exist in every team, the Intelligent Team setup needs to be able to address them because they are functioning in a self-managed environment. The following sections will provide recommendations about teamwork pitfalls.

TRUST

Trust is a key success factor in the team and more so in an Intelligent Team. Because team members do not have the constant supervision of a single person, they have to be able to trust each other and rely on each other more than any other team or situation. While setting up a team, the leaders should make sure that team members feel comfortable and vulnerable in sharing their ideas, expertise, and feelings freely, encourage each member to watch for members who will not do the same, and invite them to be part of the team fully engaged.

CONFLICTS

Conflicts and disagreements are sure to happen in any team, but Intelligent Teams are a bit different. In a traditional team, team members may avoid conflict, especially if it is with the manager, or a prominent member, leaving unresolved emotions that will eventually end up materializing in work performance. If the conflict is with another member, they may feel comfortable approaching the team lead or manager to discuss the matter toward resolution. If no proper action is taken, the team members will do the same behavior and start segregating themselves from the team.

In Intelligent Teams, it may be easier to bring up issues, and there will be more in the beginning of teamwork (more storming based on Tuckman's model). Hence, the team setup should normalize these extra conflicts and encourage conversations. Conflicts will materialize explicitly or implicitly. Hostilities in conversation, sidebar discussions, or body language are explicit forms. When observed, team members should bring it into conversation and talk it through.

Implicit conflicts where a team member hides their dissatisfaction will be harder to detect. It may show itself in undermining the solutions or decisions made by the team. The recommendation is to have Delphi voting or checkpoints within the team so everyone can share their true opinions. Eventually, after team members work together for a while and gain each other trust, differences in opinion are accepted as a norm and will be discussed directly.

COMMITMENT AND ACCOUNTABILITY

If the organization makes everything clear and avoids ambiguous approaches and promises, then there are much fewer reasons for lack of commitment. This is why **Strategy & Goals Principle** is a fundamental component of Intelligent Teams. The company leaders have to provide clear goals and objectives for the team and help transform them into KPIs that each team needs to meet. They also have to set up a reward system for succeeding in achieving the said goals. Here, Intelligent Team has an advantage: the full engagement of team members and the pleasant sense of belonging will push the team to achieve its goals.

Low standards in work will lead people to avoid accountability. With synergy elevated and augmented by an Intelligent Team, this typical drawback of traditional teamwork is addressed as well. The company leaders should try to increase the chances of success by providing quality services to the employees, regardless of the team settings. However, once externalities have been taken care of, Intelligent Team will be more efficient than other team settings, due to following *Collective Response Principle*, *Participation Principle*, and *Ownership Principle*. Inattention to results is usually caused by status and ego, but it is not a problem in an Intelligent Team because team members get past these drawbacks faster and get to perform earlier and with higher resolution.

GROUPTHINK

As mentioned earlier, groupthink is a phenomenon that can happen potentially in every team. My research didn't show an elevated amount of groupthink in the self-managed teams. However, the Intelligent Team model thrives on getting away from groupthink toward teamthink by appreciating differences between team members (*Member Difference Principle*) while respecting what each individual can bring to the table (*Experience Principle*). With full engagement through *Participation and Ownership Principles* and time allowance for the discovery of choices (*Choice Discovery Principle*), the Intelligent Team setup provides the tool for the team to avoid groupthink and move toward teamthink.

FEAR OF DECISION-MAKING

This is perhaps one of the most important differences between Intelligent Team and other setups. Everyone in the team is part of the decision-making process. Company leaders should try to minimize the fear of making wrong decisions in Intelligent Teams by instigating the trust they have in the team and making it easier for them to accept the possibility of making mistakes. A recommendation here is that the team revisits their decision after a while and uses the Problem Breakdown Principle to make the decisions into smaller units of work, so when and if they have to change it, the amount of rework is minimal. This can be, in fact, a strength point for Intelligent Teams, as we see companies go too far with certain decisions by top leaders' complacency, leading to major financial/reputational disasters. Ego has been defused in Intelligent Team, so corrective actions come naturally and early.

Chapter 10

From Manager/Team Lead to Facilitator

The role of the manager or team lead goes through a major change in Intelligent Teams, and maybe that is one of the most fundamental features of these types of teams: From a work function point of view, everyone is a core part of all the processes, in terms of teamwork, ownership, delivery, and decision-making. Instead, the lead or manager transforms into a facilitator, from a decision-maker to a decision architect. The facilitator works with organizational leaders to set up the team and make sure the multiple Intelligent Teams under their supervision can function at the best state of possibilities. A facilitator is the one who trains the team members and prepares them to function as an Intelligent Team.

LEADERSHIP STYLE

As the team doesn't have a leader, it functions based on expectations provided by the organization and channeled through the facilitators during quarterly inputs of goals and objectives. The facilitator helps with establishing the processes and encourages the principles of the Intelligent Team to become the norm. The role of the facilitator diminishes as the team matures, and depending on the underlying business, it may get limited to coordination with organizational leaders for setting and digesting strategy setting.

TEAM SETUP

Peter Drucker, a prominent management theorist, has suggested that the most important decision is not made by the team but by the manager, who sets how the team will make decisions.

A key element in setting up the team, especially an Intelligent Team, is to instigate the concepts and to let the team members know clearly this is a new setup they may not have seen before. The philosophy of the Intelligent Team is unique. It advocates team rituals versus self-achievements. It is about stepping up, feeling the responsibility, and full engagement. It is also

DOI: 10.1201/9781003527206-14

recommended to have frequent connections with the clients to make sure priorities are aligned.

SETUP COMMUNICATIONS CHANNELS

Communications always play a key role in the success of the teams. For the success of the Intelligent Team and in accordance with intelligent swarms, the members should be able to use simple ways of communicating important messages.

In nature, we see this simplicity in various forms: the frequency and intensity of emitting light in fireflies, the posture to show the level of aggressiveness in monkeys and gorillas, or the movement of tails and angle of raised feathers in many species of birds, and color change in fish species.

Communication is so important that 90% of the success is associated with how well the team members communicate with each other. Part of the team setup needs to be about how exactly and through what systems and what channel, and more specifically, what information needs to be provided. Each team member should follow the agreements of communication and post relevant information on time.

Another notable point to remember in setting up communications is finding a proper balance of frequency and details, specially when the team members want to communicate their ideas. There has to be one place for detailed information, like a document repository or Wiki page, and other types of messages should be a summary of that with a reference to the source. For example, if a team member is following the Choice Discovery Principle and has come up with an option for a decision, a detailed page should elaborate on that if needed, and a summary, like a 1–2 paragraph overall, should be used in discussions. Some people used to employ the motto "You cannot overcommunicate" to emphasize more information cannot hurt. That is not true. Too much communication will lead the messages to be ignored, and too few may not contain adequate information or bring about the importance of the message. Team members have to work together to find the right communication cadence.

TRAINING

Training of team members in an Intelligent Team is done through sharing of the ideas in this book and the principles of Intelligent Teams. The main messages that have to be passed to the team members are the ones elaborated in this part of this book, and of course, reading the book should establish the fundamental concepts of Intelligent Team. Besides that, facilitated sessions covering the following activities are recommended.

Activity	
Name	Introduction
Purpose	Practice short communications
Preparation	Team members prepare a short description of themselves that includes their background, technical knowledge, experience, interests, and some interesting nonwork facts about themselves.
Performing	All team members take time to write down their short descriptions.
Post activity	Team members are asked to review how they'd present, an elevator-pitch style. The goal is to make it interesting to listen to.

Activity	
Name	Team Building
Purpose	Team members to know each other, active listening
Preparation	Everyone provides a short description of their background, knowledge, experience, and hobbies.
Performing	All team members provide their summary.
Post activity	Team members are encouraged to converse with each other, talk about their experiences, and get acquainted.

Activity	
Name	Understanding Intelligent Team
Purpose	Team members to understand the concepts behind Intelligent Teams
Preparation	The facilitator provides a description of what an Intelligent Team is and how it can help improve team performance.
Performing	After the description is provided, the facilitator asks a few questions about Intelligent Team and encourages further questions from team members.
Post activity	Team members are encouraged to give further thoughts about Intelligent Team and discuss within the team.

Activity	
Name	Intelligent Team Principles
Purpose	Team members to learn about Intelligent Team Principle
Preparation	A handout containing a 2-page summary of Intelligent Team Principles is provided to team members.
Performing	Team members are asked to review the summary and ask questions about each principle.
Post activity	The facilitator emphasizes that principles have to be learned and practiced in everything that the team does until they become second nature to everyone.

Activity	
Name	Decision-making
Purpose	Familiarize the team with the decision-making process in Intelligent Teams.
Preparation	Provide a one-page handout containing the flow chart of decision-making in Chapter 11.
Performing	Present decision-making process (use Chapter 11 as needed). Ask team members to see how much of the process they had followed in a recent decision.
Post activity	Ask team members to discuss the process and ask questions.

Activity	
Name	Upcoming Decision
Purpose	Practice Intelligent Team decision-making process
Preparation	N/A
Performing	Ask team members to use what they have learned in the "Decision-Making" activity to discuss an upcoming decision they may need to make. Allow the team to discuss and ask questions.
Post activity	Ask members to debrief and see where in the process they might be struggling with.

Activity	
Name	Promote Autonomy
Purpose	Emphasize that Intelligent Team's decisions, planning, and so on are done within the team.
Preparation	Review Intelligent Team Principles, focusing on autonomy aspects.
Performing	Ask the team members to discuss any potential fears or risks they see in working in an autonomic state. Address the concerns by providing material on fears of decision-making in Chapter 9 and derisking decisions in Chapter 11.
Post activity	Team members are encouraged to converse with each other and feel comfortable with the autonomy they can enjoy in an Intelligent Team setting.

Activity	
Name	Strategic Alignment
Purpose	Encourage team members to understand corporate strategy and how it relates to their work.
Preparation	Work with the organization's leader to clarify how strategic goals and objectives align with Intelligent Team's work and expectations.
Performing	Provide strategic goals and objectives to the team. Start a discussion of what they mean to team members and how they can be achieved. Emphasize **Strategic & Goals Principles** and how the **Watch Principle** has to be applied to remain in alignment with strategic goals.
Post activity	Ask the team to review their current plan and rethink the priorities if needed.

Activity	
Name	Conflict Management
Purpose	Explaining how to deal with conflicts within the team without a supervisor or facilitator
Preparation	Review the "Conflict" section in Chapter 9.
Performing	Let team members know that the existence of conflict is a natural part of teamwork. The focus should be on the problem and not the person. Explain by reviewing the **Member Difference Principle**. Ask the team to be on the watch for conflicts between members and call out to discuss and resolve them. Ask the team members to feel comfortable bringing conflicts forward and not shy away from them.
Post activity	Team members to approach other team members that they had conflicts before and see how they can resolve it and could have resolved it using Intelligent Team Principles.

Activity	
Name	Change Management
Purpose	Prepare the team to manage changes
Preparation	Changes are, of course, allowed, and if the team has been set up to have a dotted link to clients, then they can control a customer-oriented list of priorities and manage the changes accordingly.
Performing	Ask the team how they expect changes may happen, that is, sources of change. Review Watch and Strategy & Goals Principles. Ask the team if they are connected with their client base and how their priorities may affect the team's plan.
Post activity	Ask the team members to have discussions within to be able to adapt to changes, especially when coming from the clients.

Chapter 11

Decision-Making

Decision-making is a relatively new term in business. Before, it was mostly used in public administration. Businesses used to "allocate resources" or "follow directions by managers." History has taught us many things about how to make a decision, and some stories have exemplified new approaches or intensity of certain decisions. In a famous story, in 333 BCE, Alexander was presented with a legendary knot on an oxcart, which was said to have been placed by the king of Phrygia. The legend said that whoever was able to untie this knot, known as the Gordian Knot, would be destined to be the ruler of Asia. Alexander didn't try to untie it and instead cut it through with his sword. Since then, the event has symbolized making tough decisions and solving hard problems with bold moves (Figure 11.1).

In another story, during the late Roman Republic, governors of Roman provinces were appointed by the Senate. In 49 BCE, Julius Caesar, who was the governor of a region ranging from southern Gaul to Illyricum, was ordered to disband his army and return to Rome. He disobeyed and marched toward Rome. At that time, the river Rubicon marked the main territory of Rome, and no armies were allowed to enter it, so when Caesar crossed the river, it was a point of no return, declaring himself against the Senate. This story and the phrase "crossing the Rubicon" have come to mean making a decision that will make changes that will not be reversed easily (Figure 11.2).

There are many ways to make a decision. Hence the team setup has to show the options to the Intelligent Team members and help to decide how they want to make decisions.

Let's look at a popular method devised by Vroom and Yetton (1973). Answering a few questions will determine the best decision style, one of the five provisioned in this particular model:

- Autocratic (A1): The leader is the one making the decision with no consultation with the team.
- Autocratic (A2): The leader consults with the team, but the decision comes from themselves without informing the group.

DOI: 10.1201/9781003527206-15

Figure 11.1 Alexander cuts through the Gordian Knot

Figure 11.2 Cesar crosses the Rubicon

- Consultative (C1): The leader consults with the team but makes the decisions for the team.
- Consultative (C2): The leader consults with the team and listens to opinions and suggestions. The difference with C1 is that suggestions from the team may be considered.

- Collaborative (G): The leader shares the decision-making process with the team and supports the team in making the decision to come up with the best option supported by all team members.

The model works based on the aforementioned decision-making approaches and the questions it asks. For example, if the quality of the decision is not important and also team commitment to the decision is not important, then the leader can make the decision A1. See the chart given in Figure 11.3 for a complete list of questions and recommended decision-makers. For our Intelligent Team model, all the decisions are made by the group, so even if the team wants to leave a question to a subgroup or an individual, the team makes a quick decision about that as well.

As you can see, it can become complicated. What I am offering here is the simplification of the decision by making all team members care about the outcomes, thus eliminating A1, A2, C1, and C2.

In following the patterns of intelligent swarms, we can provide simple guidelines to the team members. There is a philosophical principle called Occam's razor (or Ockham). William of Occam was a student of logic in the

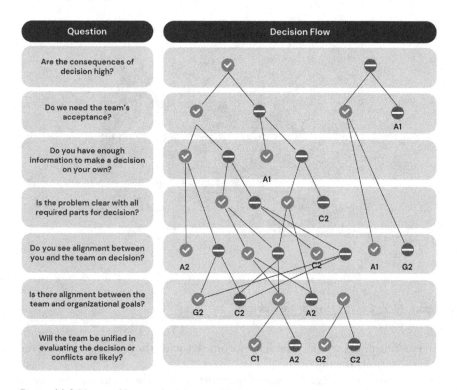

Figure 11.3 Vroom-Yetton decision-making tree

14th century who made this principle well known. It states that the simplest theory that explains all the evidence is the best theory. With the same notion, the best decision is one that covers all the evidence available.

MAKING A DECISION BY TEAM

Our Intelligent Team follows a certain procedure to make decisions. These steps ensure that it is considered, and we can get to the best decision possible given the circumstances.

What circumstances? The reality is that making decisions is not easy! First, decisions imply that the team chose to do something and not something else. This means the team gave up on the possibilities and potential advantages of another choice. In decision textbook language, the team decided that the "utility" of the option selected was better than all other options.

In the context of decision-making, utility refers to the benefit of an option. We need to define what we call the utility of a decision and then compare the result of each option's utility to see which one provides the best amount of benefit. Hence, when we choose to do something, we are really saying that the utility of that is better than all other things we could choose.

For example, if the team wants to decide what to build next, the team members may set the utility to be the importance of the next part and if it makes building the next parts easier. In a medical care team, if they are looking for a diagnosis, they may choose to run a test that answers more questions than other tests and, hence, will have the highest utility. A construction team may decide to start the next steps in parallel to speed up the build. A software team may choose the utility to build a common code that they can reuse in multiple places and give higher utility value to those particular codes.

These examples are all simple and based on one criterion. Usually, there are more! For example, the team members may face customer-driven deadlines, availability of resources, or market pressure. Or even simpler, the utility itself may have complexity, and many technical factors need to be considered.

Utility, however simple or complex, defines how the team should decide. Team members want to choose the option with higher utility. The biggest challenge that decision-making presents is uncertainty: we don't always have all the details we need to make a decision. Hence, we need to combine our decision-making approach with risks imposed by the unknowns.

We must understand how to manage the risks associated with the decisions. Attitude toward risk-taking has layers: it can be a team member, team, or organizational level, each influencing decisions in different ways.

Once we decide how to deal with risk, we can choose the best option available to us. If the probability of the unknown aspects of the options available is known, then we can calculate the value of the utility by multiplying the probability and face value of the option. Sometimes, we use a decision tree to show various options and branch out based on further options and possibilities. It can get complicated very quickly, but with the help of intelligent swarms, we can get good results easier. Still, just to be complete, here are various methods of applying the information given earlier depending on risk appetite:

1. Maximax: this approach involves selecting an option that provides a maximum of the best possible outcome. It is an optimistic or risk-taking approach.
2. Maximin: this method leans toward an option that provides the maximum or minimum payout options. It is a pessimistic approach when the team favors a safe option even if it doesn't include higher possible outcomes.
3. Minimal regret: the team should use this approach if the risk is neutral. Regret here refers to opportunity loss if the wrong option is selected. We choose an option that minimizes the regret.

What intelligent swarms teach us is that we can rely on the support of everyone in the team (*Ownership Principle*) and break down the problems into more manageable parts (*Problem Breakdown Principle*). Decisions will carry fewer risks in that case, with the option of revisiting after a short while for making corrective actions or even reversing the decision. Given the short amount of time given to the potential "wrong" option, the rework will be minimal.

Everyone on the team should vote (*Ownership Principle*). Everyone should have an opinion about how they will be contributing to this decision becoming successful (*Participation Principle*). After initial detailing of the situation (*Problem Breakdown Principle*), if the team members think that they have to discuss things further, then the team will decide to go into a few smaller groups to investigate the matters further (*Subteam Principle*). This will help these subteams to find potential better options (*Choice Discovery Principle*).

Another pre-decision setup that the Intelligent Team has to prepare for is the voting mechanism. When all the options are determined, the team gathers to review and discuss the options with all team members (*Choice Discussion Principle*). The team uses one of the options for voting. The team can decide which method to use all the time or, depending on the situation, just quickly discuss which approach makes sense in a particular case. Here are some of the voting options available:

- Consensus: A decision is made when all the members agree on a solution or option. Perhaps the most famous application of consensus is in the Jury system, where all 12 of the members have to agree (although that rule may also vary case by case). There are variations in the consensus approach, like consensus minus 1 or minus 2, that allow a semi-consensus decision despite one or two votes against the ruling.
- Majority: The most commonly used approach in voting is the majority. The team may decide to set various success thresholds or a supermajority for a decision to pass, such as 90%, 75%, 60%, and so on.

To avoid influencing team members, the team may set the vote to be in Delphi mode, in which the casting of the votes is done in secret. Also, the team may decide to run a particular decision by dotmocracy (or dot-voting). This is usually in cases where there are more than a few options available, and the team is trying to choose multiple top items or narrow down first. Each team member is provided with a few "dots" or stickers they can attach to the options they like. Each member will receive a few 3–5 if we have more than 10 options. There may be a rule in place that each member can add only one dot to each option or freely add all of the dots to the most important item in their mind.

A keynote here is based on principles of intelligent swarms; the team must try to increase the strength of decisions. I am not suggesting consensus all the time, but a strong supermajority is definitely recommended. In making any decisions, the Intelligent Team considers the *Strategy & Goal Principle* and plans to function based on the *Collective Response Principle*. With a strong vote, following the *Ownership Principle* becomes easier, and with all other principles in the decision-making group of principles, we can get close to the best decision every time. Following the *Watch Principle* will allow them to reevaluate their decisions earlier to avoid too much rework if a corrective action is required.

Figure 11.4 will help to visualize the Intelligent Team decision-making approach and covers most of what the team needs to do without including too many details that will make it hard to use:

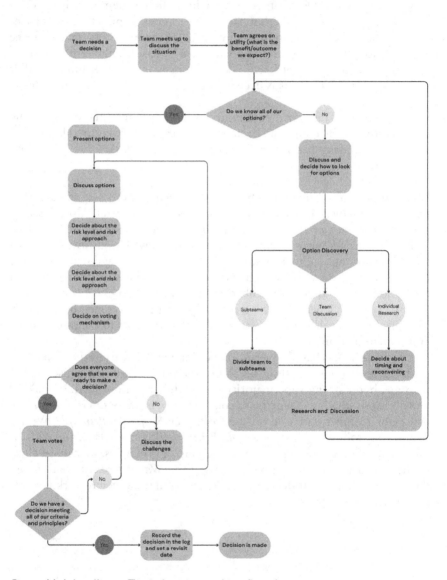

Figure 11.4 Intelligent Team decision-making flowchart

Chapter 12

Benchmarking

Intelligent swarms do what they need to, to survive. The reason we are interested in that is the success of their methods, to work with each other for all to benefit. They approach survival in different ways, sometimes demonstrating it all in one simple frame. Stripped catfish (shown in Figure 12.1) is known to swim in a swarm to give it a scary look, while the ones on top of the swarm stand watch and the ones at the bottom peck on the seabed for nutrition. They rotate as they move, so in the end, they all get a chance to eat and help protect each other in the process.

Knowing the overall strategy, the big picture, will be important for the team to be able to align its decisions and actions better (*Strategy & Goal Principle*). It will result in better outcomes, higher customer satisfaction, and improved team morale. Kaplan and Norton (1992) gave us one of the widely used methods for measuring performance, the balanced scorecard (BSC).

BSC is a simple method for transforming vision into four important aspects of implementing the strategy: translating what it means for customers, internal business processes, learning and growth, and, of course, financial stance. For each of these, we break down the answer to the question of "Where do we want to be with respect to each aspect?" into one or more objectives, and for each objective, we are going to set how we measure the progress or achievement of it, what our targets would be, and what initiatives we will run toward the said objectives.

Each of these aspects would be documented on a separate page or card (hence the term *scorecard*) as shown in Figure 12.2:

The bottom line is that each team member should have a clear understanding of how their success is going to be measured. For a software team, number of improvements, new functionality, and what size, over a certain period, are the norms. For a team of mechanics, how many cars are to be fixed after the initial evaluation has been completed and categorized based on agreed-upon measures; for a medical team, how many patients and at what severity of illness the team cares for. All of these "main" outcomes, along with how much team members elevated and enjoyed doing their work and how much the team learned to be better, will lead to financial results,

DOI: 10.1201/9781003527206-16

Figure 12.1 Stripped Catfish demonstrates a simple yet effective swarm intelligence

Figure 12.2 A typical set of goals for Balanced Score Card

and hence the four desired outcomes in the Balanced Score Card, a High Performing Team, or, as we call it, Intelligent Team.

CLOSURE

This book is the first in its approach to combining the potential power of intelligent swarms in managing teams. There are lots of potentials that still need to be explored; however, I hope this was a good starting point for this fabulous interdisciplinary field. It is definitely a shortcut to be able to set up teams based on what nature can teach us.

References

Arrow, K. J. (2012). *Social choice and individual values* (Vol. 12). Yale University Press.

Bandura, A. (1979). Self-referent mechanisms in social learning theory. *American Psychologist, 34*, 439–441. https://psycnet.apa.org/doi/10.1037/0003-066X.34.5.439.b

Deci, E. L. (1971). Effects of externally mediated rewards on intrinsic motivation. *Journal of Personality and Social Psychology, 18*(1), 105–115. https://doi.org/10.1037/h0030644

Deci, E. L., & Ryan, R. M. (2012). Motivation, personality, and development within embedded social contexts: An overview of self-determination theory. In R. M. Ryan (Ed.), *The Oxford handbook of human motivation* (pp. 85–107). Oxford University Press.

Dingsøyr, T., Fægri, T. E., Dybå, T., Haugset, B., & Lindsjørn, Y. (2016). Team performance in software development: Research results versus agile principles. *IEEE Software, 33*(4), 106–110. https://doi.org/10.1109/MS.2016.100

Drias, Y., & Pasi, G. (2016). Web information foraging. *IIR*. https://pdfs.semanticscholar.org/7e9b/bd633351f75a2f2d2371b6b86f7d3559346c.pdf?_ga=2.187213224.1003837569.1581207766-1770707167.1572287587

Dybå, T., Dingsøyr, T., & Moe, N. B. (2014). Agile project management. In G. Ruhe & C. Wohlin (Eds.), *Software project management in a changing world* (pp. 277–300). Springer.

Ghasab, M. A. J., Khamis, S., Mohammad, F., & Fariman, H. J. (2015). Feature decision-making ant colony optimization system for an automated recognition of plant species. *Expert Systems with Applications, 42*, 2361–2370. https://doi.org/10.1016/j.eswa.2014.11.011

Hughes, R., Ginnett, R., & Curphy, G. (2009). *Leadership: Enhancing the lessons of experience* (6th ed.). McGraw-Hill Irwin.

Ismail, A. R., Desia, R., & Zuhri, M. F. R. (2015). The initial investigation of the design and energy sharing algorithm using a two-way communication mechanism for swarm robotic systems. In S. Omar, W. Suhaili, & S. Phon-Amnuaisuk (Eds.), *Computational intelligence in information systems* (pp. 61–71). Springer.

Janis, I. L. (1971). Groupthink. *Psychology Today, 5*(6), 43–46. https://doi.org/10.1109/EMR.2008.4490137

Kaplan, R. S., & Norton, D. P. (1992). *The balanced scorecard: Measures that drive performance*. Harvard Business Review.

Kauffeld, S. (2006). Self-directed work groups and team competence. *Journal of Occupational and Organizational Psychology, 79*(1), 1–21. https://doi.org/10.1348/096317905X53237

Lee, M. Y., & Edmondson, A. C. (2017). Self-managing organizations: Exploring the limits of less-hierarchical organizing. *Research in Organizational Behavior, 37,* 35–58. https://doi.org/10.1016/j.riob.2017.10.002

Lee, S. T., Chae, J., Uyen, N. B. T., Gim, G., & Kim, J. B. (2016). A study of group-think in online communities. *Advanced Science and Technology Letters, 126.* https://doi.org/10.14257/astl.2016.126.23

Lee, Y. T., & Paunova, M. (2017). How learning goal orientation fosters leadership recognition in self-managed teams: A two-stage mediation model. *Applied Psychology, 66,* 553–576. https://doi.org/10.1111/apps.12101

Liff, S., & Gustavson, P. (2016). Designed for success: How building a team of leaders transformed a company. *Global Business and Organizational Excellence, 35*(4), 17–27. https://doi.org/10.1002/joe.21681

Marshall, J. A., Brown, G., & Radford, A. N. (2017). Individual confidence-weighting and group decision-making. *Trends in Ecology & Evolution, 32,* 636–645. https://doi.org/10.1016/j.tree.2017.06.004

Miller, J. H., & Page, S. E. (2009). *Complex adaptive systems: An introduction to computational models of social life* (Vol. 17). Princeton University Press.

Moe, N. B., Dingsøyr, T., & Dybå, T. (2008, March). Understanding self-organizing teams in agile software development. In *Software engineering, 2008: ASWEC 2008. 19th Australian conference on* (pp. 76–85). IEEE. https://doi.org/10.1109/ASWEC.2008.4483195

Moe, N. B., Dingsøyr, T., & Dybå, T. (2009). Overcoming barriers to self-management in software teams. *IEEE Software, 26*(6). https://doi.org/10.1109/MS.2009.182

Nozari, M., & Shuttler, R. (2021). Biomimicking as a method for self-managed teams. *International Journal of Development Research, 11*(7), 48838–48848.

Parker, D., Holesgrove, M., & Pathak, R. (2015). Improving productivity with self-organised teams and agile leadership. *International Journal of Productivity and Performance Management, 64*(1), 112–128. https://doi.org/10.1108/IJPPM-10-2013-0178

Paunova, M., & Lee, Y. T. (2016). Collective global leadership in self-managed multi-cultural teams: The role of team goal orientation. In J. S. Osland, M. E. Mendenhall, & M. Li (Eds.), *Advances in global leadership* (pp. 187–210). Emerald Group.

Seeley, T. D. (2010). *Honeybee democracy.* Princeton University Press.

Simard, M., & Lapalme, J. (2019, January). Self-organizing is not self-managing: A case study about governance challenges in an Agile IT unit and its scrum projects. In *Proceedings of the 52nd Hawaii international conference on system sciences* (pp. 6539–6548). http://hdl.handle.net/10125/60088

Solansky, S. T. (2008). Leadership style and team processes in self-managed teams. *Journal of Leadership & Organizational Studies, 14,* 332–341. https://doi.org/10.1177%2F1548051808315549

Tindale, R. S., & Kameda, T. (2017). Group decision-making from an evolutionary/adaptationist perspective. *Group Processes & Intergroup Relations, 20,* 669–680. https://doi.org/10.1177%2F1368430217708863

Tuckman, B. W. (1965). Developmental sequence in small groups. *Psychological Bulletin, 63,* 384–399. https://doi.org/10.1037/h0022100

Vroom, V. H., & Yetton, P. W. (1973). *Leadership and decision-making*. University of Pittsburgh Press.

Wageman, R. (1997). Critical success factors for creating superb self-managing teams. *Organizational Dynamics*, 26, 49–61. www.journals.elsevier.com/organizational-dynamics

Watson, W. E., Michaelsen, L. K., & Sharp, W. (1991). Member competence, group interaction, and group decision-making: A longitudinal study. *Journal of Applied Psychology*, 76, 803–809. https://psycnet.apa.org/doi/10.1037/0021-9010.76.6.803

Watson-Jones, R. E., & Legare, C. H. (2016). The social functions of group rituals. *Current Directions in Psychological Science*, 25, 42–46. https://doi.org/10.1177%2F0963721415618486

Wilson, E. O. (1978). *Sociobiology*. Harvard University Press.

Yeatts, D. E., Hyten, C., & Barnes, D. (1996). What are the key factors for self-managed team success? *Journal for Quality and Participation*, 19(3), 68. http://asq.org/pub/jqp/index.html

Index

Printed in the United States
by Baker & Taylor Publisher Services

Printed in the United States
by Baker & Taylor Publisher Services